ETHICAL BEHAVIOR
in American Local Governments

Gerry Neumark

innovativeink
PUBLISHING
A Division of Kendall Hunt

Cover image courtesy of Shutterstock.com

www.innovativeinkpublishing.com
Send all inquiries to:
4050 Westmark Drive
Dubuque, IA 52004-1840

This book is dedicated to

Ella and Hudson Neumark

Two wonderful grandchildren.

CONTENTS

INTRODUCTION

The appraisal of governments in this country (or perhaps in the entire free world) including our municipalities cannot be much lower. Stop for a moment and think about this: if you were to give a letter grade to your local government what would it be? Without a serious bit of research, I suspect very few of you would give your local government an A.

But it does not have to be this way. There many well run ethical local governments in the United States. The purpose of *Ethical Behavior in American Local Governments* is to give the readers an honest close look into the ethics and ethical behavior in our local governments from a series of unique points of view and let you come to your own conclusions. The book is intended to go beyond simply defining what is and what is not ethical. For example, public ethics and ethical behavior are examined from such perspectives as civic virtue, public organizational leadership, public organizational culture, interest group pressures, delivery of social services, technology, local neighborhoods, and the history of local ethical policies.

Although the emphasis is on local governments, many of these concepts apply to our states and federal governments. Examples are included for all three levels because ethical policies in all the levels have direct consequences for our own local governments.

Ethical behavior in American Local American Governments is intended for those who plan a career in local government, or who may already be working in local governments. The book also serves as a resource for instructors of American local government from high school through university courses. Finally, the book was written for any private citizen who has a deep interest in their local governments and public ethics.

The real strength of *Ethical Behavior in the Local* Government is that it serves to point out not only the obvious, but some of the not so obvious "pitfalls" for public employees who may not be completely familiar with some of the more subtle unethical public ethical behaviors. By pointing out some poor decisions public employees sometimes make, even without realizing that they may be unethical, the book can serve the purpose of saving you from some of the same unfortunate decisions. In addition to dealing with local ethical problems, *Behavior in the Local Government* also allows those who may not be in public service but care about local government enough to better understand how American municipalities function.

There are several important threads found throughout this book. The first is what I call "The Golden Rule of Public Ethics": equality and obligation are the ethical hallmark of local government and their employees. Government officials are **obligated** to treat **All** citizens equally and be given the same opportunities under the same circumstances. To do otherwise is unethical. Public employees are the servants of the people, not the other way around. Both of these imperatives are integral components of one's oath of office.

Another thread found in this book is use of the second person. I feel that it is important from time to time to talk directly to you. At those points where the word "you" is found, the purpose is to have you stop and think about the particular point being made. My intention is to place you in the book and to think about how material affects you personally. In some cases the unethical choices made by a public employee were obvious, but in others, actions are not always so black and white. Most of the direct statements to you are found after the case studies.

A thread presented throughout this book is the responsibility of the public. Citizens of a community have a major stake in making sure that their government operates fairly and ethically. Running for an election position is not the only way that the public can help produce and continue a government of which the citizens can be proud. With today's technical advances it is much easier to keep track of public officials. Stay informed, let your government officials know who you are, and keep the lines of communications open. We all have a responsibility towards maintaining ethical local government.

Finally, an important thread is for you to keep in mind that even though the book highlights some questionable behaviors and ethical dilemmas, by far most American municipalities and their employees are inexorably honest, ethical, and hard working. After all, many of you who are reading this book have chosen to be going into the public service field.

The majority of the chapters have one or more case studies. Almost all of these are based on real incidents. They are written into the book for a number of reasons: the cases are real life learning tools. They serve to emphasize the points being made, but they also to add interesting reading added to the text. Another reason for their inclusion is to make you think about real ethical dilemmas. As you will read, ethical choices of public employees are not always clear. The cases are there to have you think about what decisions you would make. They also on occasion add a bit of interest and humor to the book.

Each chapter has a series of notes. They have been written into the end of the text to clarify, give further background or add interest to a point being made in the body of the chapter without adding a great deal of extra length to the text. The notes give you your choice as to whether or not you would like to read the additional information.

There are also a list of thought and research concepts at the end of each chapter. Some are more covered and directly related to ethics in the text than others. Their purpose is to have you think about or research those ideas which appear as the most interesting to you.

Although each chapter can stand alone they are also connected to other chapters. As a result, some of the material may be repeated in one or more chapters. A small amount of redundancy is necessary.

This book is designed to allow many of the chapters to stand alone. At the same time, the chapters are all interconnected with the same three major themes. As a result, some or more of the material may be repeated in more than one chapters. The redundancy the reader may find is necessary to follow this design.

I would like to thank Angela Lampe and Lynne Rogers of the Innovative Ink division of the Kendall Hunt Publishing Company for their suggestions and encouragement. I would also like to thank Paul Farnham and David Lincove for their technical advice, particularly on referencing. Finally, I owe a debt of gratitude to the City of Atlanta Planning Advisory Board for electing me to my two terms on the Atlanta Ethics Office and Inspector General's Governing Board. My eight-year tenure on the board has been an invaluable experience for learning all about and teaching public ethics. Without my service, writing this book would have been impossible.

It is my hope that you enjoy reading but also learning from this book. I have included my email address if you have any questions or would like to discuss the ideas presented in *Ethical Behavior in American Local Governments*.

Gerry Neumark
Atlanta, Georgia   2025
drgneumark@outlook.com

WE HAVE A PROBLEM OR DO WE?

Two questions will be explored throughout this entire book. The first is, are local public employees and their expected on the job behaviors different than those of private employees? (Note 1) And what kinds of ethical behavior do we as the public expect from our municipal governmental employees. (Note 2)

In some ways, the job of public employees is different than their private counterparts, especially in regard to ethics. Although citizens have high expectations concerning job performance as well as communication, we especially expect our officials to achieve the highest level of ethical behavior. (Arkansas State University, 2020)

In the context of public service, then, ethics are based upon morals and values judged to be universally accepted as they concern fairness and serving the public interest. (Arkansas State University, 2020). In simple English, public servants must treat their constituents fairly and **equally**. (Note 3) The fortunate thing is that by far, most public employees live up to these expectations. Some, however, do not.

Policy

As you read through the chapters, you will notice that in some cases, un-ethical behavior is not an employee's singular choice. The lack of ethics may be an actual policy component of a government organization. In order for the reader to obtain a clear understanding of what can motivate an individual to act unethically, one must also look towards an organization's policies. For the purposes of this book, public policy is defined as what an organization chooses to do or chooses not to do. (Birkland, 2016, po. 242) If a public organization chooses to make unethical decisions, a biproduct will be a higher level of employee unethical behavior. Fortunately, there will be those who will not succumb to the organizational culture.

Avoiding pitfalls

The point of this book is not just to let the reader know the various ethical pitfalls while working for our local governments, but first, how to avoid them, and how to understand the politics surrounding working in the public service. (Neumark, 2023, p.p. 191 – 215) as well as to reiterate that public employees are very much the same as those in the private sector and have the same work ethic as most Americans workers. The only differences are those connected with the circumstances of the organizations for which they work.

WHY DO SO MANY AMERICANS HAVE NEGATIVE FEELINGS TOWARDS OUR PUBLIC OFFICIALS?

So many of us have heard this all too familiar question: why is it that there seems to be more unethical behavior among local government officials and employees than those in the private sector? One possible reason why a considerable number of Americans believe this to be true may be due to the numerous media accounts about the breakdown of such public employee ethical behavior. Questionable public ethical behavior appears constantly in the media. (Imperato, 2017, p. 18) It is sometimes difficult to listen to or view an entire local newscast or read the local newspaper without a story about the wrongdoing by some public official. Media, from the electronic to the printed constantly report government of corruption which may lead the American public to think that honesty in government is non-existent. Polls seem to indicate the same thing. (Lorch, 2001, p. 388). In a recent poll, 61 percent of those interviewed believe that our government cannot be expected to be trustworthy. (Holtz, 2023) A 2017 survey found that an increasing number of Americans believe that American governments are corrupt: the numbers rose from 35 percent to 60 percent over the period of a few years. An additional 70 percent believe that their government is failing to even fight corruption. (Compliance & Ethics Professional, 2017, p. 8) It should be pointed out, however, that these statistics were a result of perception. Although in some cases perception can be just as strong as reality. These surveys may not be intended to perform thorough research into the fact of government corruption. On the other hand, perception can be as important in forming attitudes and beliefs as actual facts.

Are Public Officials really more unethical than their private counterparts? Two Views:

Sometimes a government officials will simply act unethically having nothing to do with the culture of an organization. As an example, recently, three highly placed City of Atlanta public officials from a previous mayoral administration's cabinet were found guilty of corruption, including kickbacks. (Atlanta Constitution-Journal online, 2018). A federal investigation is still ongoing, and there is a possibility that more officials may be indicted in the future possibly including the former mayor. In light of these indictments, if you were a citizen of Atlanta, would you be wondering if all of the city's public officials corrupt? Much of the media surrounding this has led many of particularly the suburban residents to believe that the entire City of Atlanta government is totally corrupt. Would the same individuals be as concerned if these kickbacks came to light in one of the private corporations? Probably not: American conventional wisdom is that politicians are a good deal worse, morally worse, than the rest of us (Walzer, 2010, p. 5).

Hart writes that this is fact, not perception: that the widespread publicity about costly ethical failures of public organizational leaders during the last quarter of the 20th century is evident that a critical problem is the scarcity of men and women of good character in the position of significant govern-mental leadership" (Hart, 1994, p. 207). It should be pointed out that Hart, however, does not offer any proof of his contention.

At the same time, there are those having the opposite view, who feel that government as a whole, while not perfect, is even more ethical than their private counterpart. For example, public officials are more transparent. Officials see that their mission is for the entire public, while viewing private companies as their duty being for a select group of shareholders. Since both sectors have differing goals, there is a different conception of what should be the ethical standards. (Delta-Esourcing, 2022)

One such obvious difference in the standards is over each other's view of equality and equity. The clear goal of a private enterprise is to sell a prod-uct at a given price point. For those who are unable or unwilling to meet the price, those consumers may either purchase substitute goods (Corpo-rate Financial Institute, nd), inferior goods (Corporate Financial Institute, nd) or none at all. From a private enterprise perspective, there is nothing unethical whatsoever about this scenario. It is how the private marketplace should operate.

The public sector has a much different ethic. As will be emphasized throughout the entire book, the bedrock of public ethics is to insure **equality** to all concerned. The inability to pay for a public service, excluding some reasonable toll goods, is not a factor in the provision of services. Equal treatment or sometimes equity of service are. (Note 4) With these differences in the ethos of private and public sectors there is no reason to believe that our local governments are automatically more unethical than private enterprises.

Perception

The public's perception of all sorts of actions and events is another reason why the too many individuals believe local governments to be general-ly unethical. Not all local citizens completely understand how our local governments work, for example. Decisions are often made under strict guidelines from city charters, as well as from other levels of government.

Local constituents may not be fully aware of all of the myriad of rules and guidelines. (Some attorneys aren't either) What may seem to be unethical is simply a matter of following the rules. Misunderstanding exacerbates perception over fact.

Although certain facts and names have been changed, Case study 1.1 looks at a real ethical dilemma from four years ago in a large American city. Is there a serious factual ethical issue among members of an important licensing board, or is the occurrence a matter of perception?

Case Study 1.1: PERCEPTION OR REALITY: THE MUNICIPAL LIQUOR LICENSE COMMISSION

The nine-member Municipal Liquor License Commission was formed in a large metropolitan city to regulate the amount of liquor as well as beer and wine licenses to package stores, grocery stores, restaurants, and bars. The other function is to sanction those institutions found guilty of violating the city's liquor license code, most of which is governed by state law. As one can imagine, the commission is always under a great deal of political pressure since a liquor license is possibly the most valuable position a restaurant, bar or package store can have. It is the very lifeblood of their existence. The opposite pressure comes from neighborhoods which prefer not to have these types of businesses in their communities.

In an upscale neighborhood in this particular city, along one of its main thoroughfares, there is an adult entertainment club. The club, "2040 Sunset Strip," has been there for twenty years and has had a relatively good relationship with the neighborhood, but in the past few years it had experienced a change in ownership. From that point on, relations between the neighborhood and club went sour. Patrons started parking all up and down the quiet nearby residential streets making noise all times of the night even beyond legal closing time, resulting in a major disturbance in the adjoining single-family streets. Loud music came from the club itself, which refused to turn down the volume. There was increasing evidence that the club was pouring beyond the legal closing time (2:00 a.m.), and possibly serving minors.

Starting about four years ago, the neighborhood filed a complaint with the Municipal Liquor License Commission. The first action of the commission was to write the club a letter asking them to be more considerate of the neighborhood. That worked for two weeks. The disturbances continued. Finally, the commission scheduled a hearing on the complaints. At the hearing the attorneys for the club asked that the hearing could be delayed in order for them to have more time to develop a defense. Although four of the nine members were not convinced, the commission voted to allow the delay. One month later, at the next regularly scheduled commission meeting, the exact same thing happened. The hearing was then delayed two more months by the same vote from the same commission members. During the third hearing the club was fined $100 for its offenses.

The problem seemed to die down for about a year, but then it mushroomed again. Once again, the neighborhood filed a complaint to the commission. It took about six months for the next hearing to be scheduled. Finally, the time came, and a more serious sanctions vote was taken. Strangely, five commissioners including the same four members who voted in favor of the delays left the room for various reasons at the point when the vote was to be taken. Since they no longer had a quorum, the meeting ended without a vote. The conflict between the club and the neighborhood continued, however.

The next hearing was scheduled to be heard at the regular commission meeting three months later. During that period of time, a more serious incident involving the club occurred. The club held a New Year's Eve party. At 2:30 a.m., the party was still going strong with plenty of noise. The police were called, but the manager of the club refused to allow the officers in saying that it is private property, and the police could not enter without a warrant. The police were able to get an emergency warrant, the manager was arrested, and the club was closed down, at least for the night. It was back in business two days later.

The commission hearing finally happened. Once again strangely enough, the same five members excused themselves for various reasons and left the hearing room. The vote never happened. It wasn't until five months later that the commission voted to close the club down for one week.

At that point, a resident of the neighborhood, who herself was on another municipal board became concerned that there may be some ethical issues. Was it just a matter of coincidence that the same liquor commission members left the meeting twice and in the end the club only received a slap on the wrist? She then decided to contact the city's ethics manager who promised a complete investigation into whether or not there were indeed some ethics violations from certain liquor commission members.

Almost a year went by, but the neighborhood resident heard nothing from the ethics manager. Finally, she contacted him again. He told the resident that the ethics investigator could find nothing amiss with those specific members as well as the entire process regarding the club, much of which was dictated by state law. As a result, the matter was put on hold.

The club finally lost its license after a series of shootings in their parking lot. But even the loss of its license is in a gray area. They simply sold their license and business to another party and the club continued to operate. Many residents of the neighborhood believe that the new owner is a shadow proprietor and that the previous owner is still calling the shots. The commission has yet to rule on this possibility.

- Was (is) there questionable ethical behavior among certain board members as well as the ethics officer? Was there a coverup? Or was it just a matter of coincidence and perception? After all there was a complete investigation by the ethic's department which itself has an outstanding reputation. You decide!

Perception may be a product of expectations. We expect a great deal from our public employees. The fact is Americans assume that public employees will treat their positions as a public trust. (Denhardt, 2013) Notice the use of the word **expectations**. Denhardt wrote this back in 2013. Over the last several years this view may be changing. Have American citizens become more cynical when it comes to our governments. Do we still hold these expectations? It may be one thing to say our governments may not be trustworthy. But have as we Americans no longer even expected them to be? Sadly, although this may be the case, as we regard our federal level elected employees, but also for the closest government to the people, the local level, (the focus of this book.) How much of this American cynicism is earned by the actual functioning of our governments, or how much is nothing more than perception? What should we the public be expecting from our local officials? Is unethical behavior nothing more than a myth? If so, why do so many Americans believe in this myth when most public employees honestly go about doing their work. (Neumark, 2002, p. 3)

Unethical or illegal?

There is still an additional reason why so many Americans seem to have a negative view of the behavior of public officials: public employee's unethical behavior does not necessarily reach the level of being illegal. The media may report an official's wrongdoing, but ethics and law are two different matters. Some unethical employees are able to get away with their conduct to the point where they are still able to retain their positions in government since they have not broken any law. These individuals may receive nothing more than a small fine. Codes of ethics are very often policy not law, and they vary from government to government even within the same state. (Neumark, 2023, p.p. 12-13) Under these circumstances, some ethical failings are difficult to sanction to the fullest extent. This is not to say that such major and obvious offences as conflict of interest, seeking to enrich one's own financial standing at the expense of taxpayers (The misuse of P-cards or flying first class to an officially sanctioned conference for examples. See Table 1.1), as well as clear corruption are not addressed by the law (Killilea, 1996, p. 5). When caught they certainly are. However, when constituents see serious or not so serious lapses of ethical behavior, they become jaded and dubious about honesty within our governmental organizations. After all, some private sector employees can get away with behaviors which although may not normally be tolerated by one's own personal code of ethics, are nevertheless not considered important.

Ethical codes and law: our private codes of ethics

It is not uncommon for Americans to inject their own personal values into their beliefs on how government should be run. One's personal ethics is a product of local social values. Whether or not a person looks at political campaigns, political decisions, legislation or policy development, ethics as social values play an important role. We often think that personal ethics (moral code) of public officials should be no different than one's own moral code (Cochran *et al*, 2006, P.3), but they are. In reality, a public code of ethics is quite circumscribed and can be vastly different from one's personal code. Of course, in reality there are elements of both. Most Americans draw a line between what we see happen in private and the very same behavior one finds in the public sector. Think about this: what would happen if there were a news story about some corporate executive using a corporate automobile for his or her own pleasure when it is clearly against company policy. Would we even care? Consider what would happen if the same scenario happened in our city's government. Would we care? Would we assume that government employees simply cheat when they can get away with it? Or would we just say that's government for you?

A sample of unethical public behaviors

Of course it is naïve to believe that all local public officials are completely ethical at all times. If that were the case ethics codes would not exist. Whether fact or perception, there are behaviors which will always be unacceptable from employees in the public sector. The following table presents a sample of some of the more common unethical behaviors sometimes found among public employees. Although most of these are directly related to public employees, some are also found in the private sector but are more tolerated. Notice that a few are less obvious than others.

- Misusing Consideration of contracts.
- Nepotism
- Using public equipment for private purposes
- Purposely ignoring the public's interests and concerns
- Conflicts of interest
- Unequal treatment of the population
- Not keeping up with the latest technology to better serve the public
- Taking gifts from prohibited sources (including entertainment tickets and preferred event seating)
- Representing private interests in government matters
- Disclosing inside privileged information
- Using paid working hours for private purposes

WHY PUBLIC ETHICAL BEHAVIOR MATTERS

Unethical behavior ultimately has its toll as it affects the politics and operations of our local governments. To the extent that the public believes that their governments are inherently unethical the effects can be quite dramatic. "Absent a strong ethics program, the entire government-community relationship suffers from the misconduct of those few unethical officials and employees." (Sengova, 2022, p. 1) How does this relationship suffer?

The following represents some of these effects:

- Decreases in voter turnout, which in turn creates the greater possibility of electing unqualified candidates
- Decreases in citizen participation in their government as well as in civic activities: why bother, the government is corrupt anyway?
- Increased questioning of the legitimacy of governmental authority
- Lack of compliance with laws, but in particular local ordinances
- Putting local economic development in doubt
- Skepticism regarding governmental actions of all types

- Decreases in public employee job satisfaction
- Makes it more difficult to hire the brightest and best professionals to serve the municipality
- Negatively affecting a community's social cohesion.
- Destroying trust in government

(Holtz, 2023)

Trust

Questioning, of course, is a vital aspect of the American open democracy. In doing so, citizens expect honest answers even though they may not agree with a government's policy position. Questioning and trust go hand-in-hand. Wechsler adds that without trust, "people tend not to participate in their government, even as voters, and they feel as if their government [is] something apart from their community…A democratic government does not thrive when there is a lack of trust in those who govern it." (2013, p.p. 4-5).

Trust in the ethical behavior among our public officials is of significant importance, not just because an ethical government looks good. Not just because an ethical government promotes pride among its citizens. But because it allows for the smooth operation of our governments on which we depend.

THE ROLE OF THE PUBLIC

Public employment as a covenant

Taking a position with a government is different in one important way than working in the private sector: every public employee, no matter which level, enters into a **public covenant** with the citizens to promote public trust (Pelissero, 2021). This covenant is there to make sure that favoritism nor discrimination exists in public service. The concept also serves to enforce our high standards which puts public employees in the constant spotlight. The covenant to which Pelissero alludes may not be written, but with all covenants there are mutual expectations, and the relationship between employees of public organizations and their constituents reflect these expectations.

Ethical behavior does not start at the point when an individual is hired, chosen, or elected. It starts from the very beginning as a part of a democratic process, including elections, and campaigns. (Pelissero 2021) This also includes the comprehensive vetting of a prospective public employee. That is the only way a democracy can function.

A two-way street

One of the purposes of this book is to paint a realistic picture about ethical behavior in our local sector and how local citizens can be, or rather should be, ensuring ethical behavior from local public officials. After all, the health of any political structure of government must rely on the highest standards of conduct from its public officials. It is up to us as citizens to not only expect the best from our public employees, but to make sure they meet our reasonable expectations. If we don't, we won't get the best of our governments. Public ethical behavior is a two-way street.

CONCLUSION

At the beginning of this chapter, we posed the question: are local government employees more unethical than those in the private sector?- There is no reason or proof to make one believe that public service workers are inherently less ethical than their private counterparts. All segments of the American workforce have their good actors but also their bad actors.

The purpose of this book is not only to obtain a deeper understanding of public ethical behavior, but to increase our knowledge of the role of local American governments in this endeavor. Also for the reader to look deeply into the give and take of the politics involved between the local governments and their codes of ethics as it affects the behavior of their employees.

We begin our journey through public employee behavior by addressing what is meant by the concept of ethics. There is clearly a close relationship between the concepts of ethics, integrity, and morality. At the same time there is a difference between public and private ethical expectations. The problem is that the two are often confused with each other.

So many Americans appear to have negative views about our public employees on all levels of American governments. Sixty to seventy percent of our citizens believe that our governments are inherently corrupt. (Compliance & Ethics Professional, 2017, p. 8; also see Lorch, 2001, p. 388) The problem is that this belief lingers without any real proof. There are, however, several reasons why this notion persists. First, the media tends to emphasize stories about corruption without making sure that their readers or viewers understand that when an individual is caught in some unethical activity, it does not reflect on all government employees. Government employees as their counterparts are by far honest and ethical hard-working individuals. Indeed, they may be your neighbors, your family, or even you.

The second reason is our own personal perception from whatever source. For many people, perception is as real as reality.

This does not mean that there are behaviors which public employees should never practice. These include such unethical choices as kickbacks, nepotism, and conflict of interest to name a few. There are individuals who engage in these, but as this book well contend, very few.

We as citizens must be concerned about unethical public employee behavior when it does occur. In those infrequent instances, it hurts both the operation of our governments as well as our confidence in how they are able to render needed services. This also goes along with perception. If we believe that our governments are failing us, indeed, in reality they are doing just that.

As you read through the remainder of this book, ask yourself a few of the following questions: is there a problem? If so, is the public organization addressing it? If not, why do we believe so? But most important of all, what can we do as citizens to make sure that our governments and their employees are always honest and very highly ethical?

NOTES

Note 1: This book is meant to concentrate on the local level of government; however from time-to-time other levels will be discussed for additional information or for comparative purposes.

Note 2: For the purposes of this book, the terms "public employee" or "public official," will designate any individual who is in a policy making position or has direct communication with the public in a local government. This includes the mayor of a city or the executive of a county down to a clerk in the water department. The behavior of an employee is more important than on which level that person may be.

Note 3: The word equally is written in bold letters. This book strongly emphasizes that equal treatment of all citizens when possible is among the most important ethical tenants of local governments and public employee ethical behavior. (See Note 4) Unfortunately, citizens as well as policy makers sometimes forget the important connection between ethics and equal treatment.

Note 4: Equity is another important value beside equity. Where equality means that all consumers of a particular public service are treated exactly the same under all circumstances, there are times where equality may not be the best solution to a service delivery problem. In the case where there may be areas of a local municipality in need of something from the government more than in another area, under those circumstances, instead of equality of that item delivered to the entire city or county, the local government provides for equity, giving the needy area a greater amount of that service. (Felbinger, 2016, 121). For example, more schools are provided in a neighborhood where there are a greater number of school age children than in than where there are fewer such younger persons. Or one finds more fire stations in older more densely populated neighborhoods than in newer areas with larger properties and modern fireproof building materials. Whether a municipality chooses an equality or equity policy, they are both important in ethical service delivery.

Note 5: We may also wish that such a covenant exists between private employees and the public, but except for obeying government regulations, ordinances, and law, private organizations are pretty much free to do as they wish. This is not to imply that these organizations do not care to serve the public. They do so by choice.

CONCEPTS FOR THOUGHT OR RESEARCH

Campaigns and elections

Codes v. law

Consideration of contract

Corruption

Democracy

Equality

Equity

Ethics

Honesty

Inferior goods

Kickbacks

Media

Perception of public corruption

Policy

Prohibited sources

Public employee behavior

Public covenant

Public trust

Social values

Substitute goods

Transparency

Trustworthy

Work ethic

REFERENCES

Arkansas State University. (2020). "The Importance of Ethics in Public Service. https://www.degree.astate.edu. Accessed: October 26, 2023.

Atlanta Journal -Constitution. (2018) "Defendants in the Atlanta Corruption Probe are Due In Court Today." www.ajc.com.defendants-atlanta-corruption-probe-court-today/fBBZmRJr)94WuQtqPoxAcP/. Accessed: August 15, 2023.

Birkland, T. A. (2016) *An Introduction to the Policy Process theories, concepts, and Models of Public Policy Making.* (4th ed.). New York: Routledge Taylor and Francis Group.

Cochran, C. E., L.C. Mayer, T. R. Carr, and N. J Cayer. (2006). *American Public Policy.* (8th ed.) Belmont, CA: Thomson Higher Education.

Compliance & Ethics Professional. (2017). "US Corruption Barometer Climbs Upward. (15, 2). P. 8.

Corporate Financial Institute. (nd) "Inferior Goods." Corporatefinancialinstitute.com/resources/economics/inferior-Goods/. Accessed: December 29, 2024.

___________. (nd) "Substitute Goods." orporatefinancialinstitute.com/resources/economics/substitute-products/. Accessed: December 29, 2024.

Delta ESourcing. (2022). https://www.delta-esourcing.com/resources/etendering-blog/2022/06/06/. Accessed: October 26, 2023.

Denhardt, K. G. (2013). "Ethics in Public Organizations." https://www.eoless.net. Accessed: August 8, 2023.

Felbinger, C. L. (2016). "The City Maintains Itself Public Works." In G. Neumark. *Citizenship In the Local Community* (3rd ed.) Dubuque, Iowa: Kendall Hunt Publishing Company.

Hart, D.K. (1994). "Administration and the Ethics of Virtue in All Things, Choose First for Good Character and then for Technical Expertise." T. L. Copper (Ed.) *Handbook of Administrative Ethics.* New York: Marcel Dekker. 107-23.

Holtz, J. (2023). "Public Trust in Government by the Numbers." *Diligent.* August 4, 2023. Imperato, G. (2017). "Meet Ana-Paola ("AP") Capaldo." *Compliance & Ethics Professional.* Vol 14, 2. P.p. 16-20.

Killilea, A. G. (1996). "Machiavelli, Bok, and Public Ethics." L. Pasquerella, A. G. Killilea, and M. Vocino (eds). *Ethical Dilemmas in Public Administration.* Westport, Connecticut: Praeger Public Press. P. p. 5 – 6.

Neumark, G. (2022). "Public Ethical Behavior a Matter of Civic Virtue." *Atlanta Ethics in Action,* (Vol 17). P.p. 3-5.

_________, G. (2023). *Civic Literacy Politics and Policy in the American City.* Dubuque, Iowa: Kendall Hunt Publishing Company.

Pelissero, J. (2021). "What is Government Ethics?" www.scu.edu/government-ethics/resources/what-is-government-ethics/ Accessed: September 5, 2023. What-is-government-ethics/ Accessed: September 6, 2023.

Sengova, J. M. (2019). 'City of Atlanta Board of Ethics 2018 Annual Report. P. 1.

Walzer, M. (2010). "Political Action: The Problem of Dirty Hands." *Public Ethics (Ed.* R. Bellamy and A. Palumbo.) Burlington, VT: Ashgate Publishing Company. 3-23

CIVIC VIRTUE AND PUBLIC ETHICS

2

INTRODUCTION

In many ways, public ethics and civic virtue (Rohr, 1989) are synonyms. In this chapter we will take a closer look at both and how they interact with each other. The chapter will also take a closer look at the difference between public and private ethics. Where civic virtue defines public ethics, it has little connection with what private individuals consider ethical. We all have our moral codes, but what our governments consider ethical may be very different.

PUBLIC

The chapter begins by defining "public." When one hears the term public or public sector, many of us assume we are referring just to a government. This is the most frequent use of the term. For the purposes of this book, a broader use of the notion of the public sector will be used. Thus includes, not only government and government employees, but also, "all institutions and organizations that ... have public obligations." (Frederickson, 2013, p. 9) This includes some non-profits as well as vendors which have established partnerships with governments. Although corruption can happen on all levels of government, the concentration as it will be throughout the remainder of the book is on the local level of American governments. It is important to remember that not only are our local governments the closest to the people, but they are the ones which most affect everyday life in this country. (Newman, 2016). If unethical local governments and government employees' behavior is to happen the direct effect will be mostly felt by the local populations.

Non-profits and vendors are included because there is not always a clear boundary between public and private. Take for example a case of nepotism from the owner of a private company under contract to a municipality to be the sole supplier of water and sewer services to a given city. Is this a public or a private unethical act? Public and private ethical expectations are not always the same. This point will be made clear though out this chapter.

PERSONAL ETHICS

Defining "ethics" can be a bit tricky. In a sense, everyone has his or her own conception. And although there are as many definitions as there are individuals, there is one element of public ethics which is universal. It is perhaps the most important component of what we consider good government: ethical behavior promotes trust in public service. (Downe, Cowell, and Morgan, 2016)

One should also keep in mind that even though in the end a code of public ethics may be quite different than one's personal codes, they may very well be interconnected. Without personal ethical codes, public codes would have no basis. Although this chapter concentrates on public behaviors, what a society determines as acceptable cannot be completely separated from what individuals in a society believe is acceptable.

For the purpose of presenting a clear definition of ethics, it will be helpful to look at some of the thinking regarding both private and public ethics. TheFreeDictionary.com defines ethics as, "a system of moral principles as well as rules of conduct with respect to the rightness and the wrongness of actions." It is a civil code of *behaviour* considered correct" (2013). This definition applies to one's private as well as public behavior. Our ethical behavior reflects how we act when no one is watching.

Rohr adds the concept of moral character (morality) to Free Dictionary definition. Ethical behavior goes beyond simple right or wrong actions, ethics reflects a deeper societal belief in morality (1989, p 2): I may steal a cookie from the cookie jar, but no one is going to call this a moral failing. Or I may rob a bank which of course is a serious legal breach, and the culprit is subject to sever sanctions, but is it morally wrong?

In the United States the belief is that for a government employee to skim tax money off the top is not only wrong, but also immoral, however. It is usurping what belongs to the public. Sengova (2022) believes that in some "third world" nations, this may be expected behavior, but definitely not in Western civilization.

Northouse adds the concept of values as a guideline to establish what is right and wrong and moral. Which ways of acting are important to Americans? How does society determine what is right or wrong, especially in light of all the differing cultural beliefs of the entire 300 million plus individuals in our population? Thus, what is ethical is determined by the kinds of values and morals an individual or society finds desirable or appropriate. One can think of values as a system of rules and principles which serve to guide individuals or a society in making decisions about what is right or wrong and good or bad in various situations. (Northouse 2007, p. 342).

Another element of ethics is one's personal character. A widely accepted definition of personal character is the "six pillars of character." They include:

- Trustworthiness
- Respect
- Responsibility
- Fairness
- Caring
- And involved citizenship (Josephson Institute 2022).

Putting these concepts together

The common thread throughout all of these definitions is ethics are those actions that live up to a society's moral principles, where conduct is consistent with the rules of that society and where decisions about what is right and wrong, good and bad are made in the context of honesty and trustworthiness. Ethics, morals, personal character, values, and integrity are all closely related.

Defining ethics is the difficult task of putting all of these concepts together in our diverse society. For the purposes of this book, the best definition of ethics is the sum of all of the different elements written above. They all point to individuals doing the right thing for the good of our society and governments. It is what individuals at a given time and place consider to be the correct mode of behavior.

PUBLIC ETHICS AND ETHICS CODES

Public ethics is about acting responsibly and professionally, incumbent on government officials and employees, following certain rules and procedures. (Wechsler, 2013, p.4). One may talk about the morals and ethics of a given community, but that does not mean that everyone shares the exact view on what constitutes ethical behavior. Ask a university student what his or her understanding of ethics means, then ask a person over sixty-five, and you are bound to get some very different answers. Most local governments in this country understand this point. A community's personal outlooks cannot always be included in a public ethics code. Governments then have developed formal specific expectations of employee ethical behavior which appeal more directly to governmental operations and goals and less on private moral convictions. At the same time, ethics codes cannot lose sight on what is a more general local sense of propriety. The one view of public ethics that all governments have in common is that public ethics is the fulfillment of the constituent's interest. It is in the best interest of all to provide public services in a fair and equitable manner. (Morgan, 1994, p. 125)

Do we even need ethics codes?

Why is it even necessary for a municipality to have ethics codes? Protecting the integrity of government, promoting the public trust, and instilling a culture of ethical behavior in city government are critical functions that require consistent and continuous education, open transparent government, and monitoring at-risk governmental functions to identify problems at an early stage. Absent a strong ethics program with clear codes, the entire government-community relationship suffers from the misconduct of some officials and employees. (Sengova, 2019, p 1).

Public ethical standards may or may not be any different than those expected from the private sector. Yet one of the important differences is that citizens have a different level of tolerance in judging the two sectors. But the public should expect the highest level of ethical behavior from those who carry out the public's business. The following is a list of some of the more common public ethical failings:

- Bribes
- Conflicts of interest
- Working for a specific candidate running for public office during working hours
- Kickbacks for letting of contracts
- Improper consideration of contracts
- Practicing partisan politics in an official neutral local government, including running for office under a partisan label (Brooke 2000, p.p. 16 – 19)
- Nepotism
- Working on private business during public working hours
- Not treating constituents completely equally
- Dishonesty in producing public documents
- Using public equipment for private purposes
- Padding expense accounts
- Using the governments p-card for private purposes
- Accepting gratuities (including gifts or tips)
- Mishandling of public funds
- Hiring without proper public notification, including failure to advertise a government's opening position

Some of these may not necessarily be crimes, but they are all unethical behavior on the part of trusted government authorities.

Clearly knowing what is or what is not public ethical behavior is important to the behavior of public employees. Ethic codes are a tool in a well-functioning government which in turn leads to a well-functioning society. Understanding the entire role of government including our own ethical expectations is vital information for an entire public, since every decision made by our leadership affects all of us, particularly on the local level since these governments are the closest to the people and have the most immediate effect on our everyday lives. (Newman, 2016)

Unethical public employee behavior is damaging. It can lead to citizens becoming jaded about the behavior of their officials with the thought: "This is just the way government is." It can cause a whole myriad of negative effects. For the local population as well as our public employees it is essential that everyone must be able to understand, recognize, and identify illegal or unethical behavior.

As an illustration of how damaging corrupt behavior can be, in one city, a particular state came very close to taking away a city's major airport because of alleged corruption of the airport's management. In the same state, another city's charter was revoked for the same reason and that city no longer exists. Finally, over a period of time several elected sheriffs in this state have been removed for their corrupt behavior. Some of these events in the one state may very well be happening throughout the country.

CIVIC VIRTUE: PUBLIC EMPLOYEES DOING THE RIGHT THING

When morality, integrity, honesty and civility from government officials are summed up one comes to the definition of **civic virtue**, a concept which should be familiar to all Americans: treat each other fairly and with civility and respect. (Note 2) For the purposes of this chapter, civic virtue and the highest level of public ethical behavior are synonymous. (Rohr, 1989, p. 285)

Confusion over civic virtue

Since civic virtue pertains to the public behavior of employees, it is not always clear whether or not a person's behavior may or not be defined as virtuous. Case study 2.1 illustrates the sometimes confusion.

CASE STUDY 2.1: THE FULTON COUNTY DISTRICT ATTORNEY'S AFFAIR

In the State of Georgia, a former president of the United States is being investigated for the possibility of interfering with and manipulating the results of the preceding presidential election outcome in that state. Because Atlanta is the capital city and is mostly located in Fulton County the job of investigating and possibly charging the former president was assigned to that county. The charges are very serious and considered a felony under state law.

After a prolonged period of time, several members of that former presidents political party were found guilty or pleaded guilty to racketeering charges (RICO). The former president himself has also been charged but his case has not yet come to trial. Whether or not one agreed with the process, it was generally accepted that the district attorney was working steadily and carefully towards building the case.

Recently it came to light that the district attorney was engaged in an affair with the chief investigator of this case. The local as well as the national broadcast and print media began to focus on the affair instead of the actual case. Ultimately, the chief investigator in question resigned.

There was never any evidence whatsoever that the relationship between the district attorney and the investigator had any effect on the process. Both were very professional in their actions regarding what one would expect in a case such as this. At no time did their relationship appear to affect the possible outcome case. From a public perspective her actions must be considered to be ethical.

But the media coverage presented a dilemma. Did the continuous coverage of the affair weaken the district attorney's ability to continue the case? Should she have recused herself even though her pursuit of the case appears to be strictly professional? In other words, did she display civic virtue while her private actions may have violated the personal ethical codes of some of the county and state residents?

This case serves to present a clear outline of the differences between private ethics codes on one hand and one's civic virtue on the other. Ultimately, the investigator resigned, and state court removed her from the case. Can one display civic virtue in a public setting but not in another?

- Was the Affair a private or public laps?
- Do you think her private behavior harmed her public duties in any way?
- If you were a public figure, would you exercise more circumscription? Or would you believe that what you do in private has no bearing on you position as a public employee?
- Do you believe that the media was unfair to the district attorney?

The ethical confusion presented by the district attorneys private behavior may not be all that uncommon. For example, a city's high level department manager is caught gambling after work hours by an unhappy whistle blower. On the private level, some, but certainly not all, would find that morally wrong. Should the manager lose his or her job? Did this person violate the city's code of ethics? Probably not. Very few, if any, municipal codes of ethics even address whether or not their employees may gamble on their own private time. The public may be unhappy regarding the "personal quality" of their top-level employees, but that is about as far as it goes. The same individuals would not even think twice if the same thing happened with a private coworker. Is the coworker without civic virtue for participating in a private poker game?

Civic virtue must be democratic

To be completely ethical, decisions rendered by our governments must be fair, impartial, and democratic. One concern arises, however, which is often related to the amount of latitude a public service provider may have: the more discretion, to make their own policies, the more likelihood biased decisions can become problematic. (Peters 2000, p. 127). This includes both public and contracted private agencies. There is nothing wrong or unethical about giving a government administrator or a contracted vendor a reasonable amount of decision making. Allowing an administrator to make his or her own decisions is fundamental to well operating governments. There must be an understanding that the amount of latitude will be used wisely.

Whether it pertains to service delivery or within the organization itself, without strong inner controls, decision making can become one sided in favor of only those who managers deem worthy of the service, leaving others out. If governments practice civic virtue, and if the public is to accept the legitimacy of decisions emanating from their government, elected, appointed as well as career officials behavior must be open and democratic.

When citizens perceive government officials' behaviors as arbitrary and at odds with democratic values, there is a loss of public ownership of those governments. If undemocratic decisions are the norm, citizens very often choose to disassociate themselves from that level of government, be it local, state, or federal (Chandler 1994, 152). The consequences of undemocratic governments have far reaching consequences for the services rendered to that community, especially with the loss of trust. Local governments are well served to keep their operations as democratic as possible. (Note 3) (Note 4)

IMPORTANT DEFINITIONS

As we continue our journey through the remainder of this book, we will point out some of the obvious or perhaps less obvious public ethical failures. We start by defining a number of important terms. "Public" refers to the public sector, including those organizations contractually connected to a specific government. It also includes all levels within in our federal system, including such governments as authorities and districts.

Personal ethics are what most individuals consider right and wrong. For the most part our ethical outlook is a combination of morals and integrity. Although it varies from person to person, almost all of us have our own set of personal ethics.

Public ethics are behaviors specific to the public sector. Since it is impossible to incorporate everyone's personal ethics into our expectations of public employee behavior, governments have come up with a list of the kinds of behaviors which either detract from or in hance their operations. These are normally called codes of ethics. Most of the codes are quite different from our personal codes. Notice that some of these violations would not be tolerated by the public while at the same time, they would be completely ignored in the private sector. On the other hand, governments cannot ignore what society regards what is or what is not ethical behavior.

The important thing is that no matter how the government or the public perceives what is right or wrong, when a government official continues doing the right thing, we call this civic virtue. (Rohr 1989) It applies to those government officials who are fair and democratic, who treat their constituents with the highest level of respect. It is what both the local citizens as well as a public organizations expect from their employees.

CONCLUSION

Chapter two connects two important aspects of public ethical behavior: public ethics and civic virtue. Both are interconnected. The chapter starts out be defining what is meant by public then personal and goes on to separate the two. Although some portions of public codes are based upon a community's understanding of morality, and acceptable behavior, they are not the same.

We then pose the question are public ethics codes even necessary. They clearly are. Well considered codes foster the constituents' trust in their local governments. They also provide an important road map for employees to follow. All together the policies and laws which make up a local government's codes of ethics are in important part of a well-functioning government

Finally, the chapter suggests that the highest form of employee ethical behavior and civic virtue are really one and the same. As this book defines all ethical behavior as a combination of morality, integrity, and honesty, when civility is added one comes up with the definition of public employee ethical behavior: civic virtue. (Rohr, 1989, p. 285)

NOTES

Note 1: How much of one's personal private ethical conduct is important in his or her public role often depends on the size and location of the local governments. Smaller municipalities in this country are more likely to include personal characteristics in their codes of ethics. Larger local governments mostly confine their code of ethics strictly to that government's public operations. (atlantaethics.org)

Note 2: Civility is simply based on what we Americans understand as the "Golden Rule": Do on to others as you would have others do on to you. How do public officials treat others including fellow employees as well as the public?

Note 3: Being as democratic as possible within a representative democracy does not negate the importance of a government's ability and necessity to make private decisions as needed. Most governments are allowed the privilege of executive sessions where private matters are discussed as dictated by state laws.

Note 4: Once again the emphasis is on local government. How the public feels about ethical issues may ultimately be a concern to the higher levels, unethical behavior among local public employees has a much more direct impact. (Newman, 2016, p.p. 143-156)

CONCEPTS FOR THOUGHTS OR RESEARCH

Civic Virtue	Morality
Civility	Personal character
Codes	Public Employees
Codes of ethics	Six pillars of character
Corruption	The "Golder Rule"
Democratic behavior	Trust in Government
Honesty	Trustworthiness'
Integrity	Values
Laws	

REFERENCES

Atlantaethics.org. (2021). www.atlantaethics.org. Accessed: July 26, 2024.

Chandler, R. C. (1994). "Deontological Dimensions of Administrative Ethics." In *Handbook of Administrative Ethics*, edited by T. L. Cooper, 147–66. New York: Marcel Dekker.

Downe, J. R Cowell, and K. Morgan. "What Determines Ethical Behavior in Public Organizations: Is it Rules or Leadership"?. (2016). https://doi.org/10.111/puar.12562. Accessed: October 11, 2023.

Josephson Institute. (2022). www.josephsoninstitute.org. Accessed: January 14, 2024.

Morgan, D. F. (1994). "Public Interest." In *Handbook of Administrative Ethics*. T. L. Cooper (ed). New York: Marcel Dekker. (P.p. 124 – 46).

Newman, H. (2016). "Citizenship in the Local Community." In G. Neumark (Ed). *Citizenship In the Local Community* (3rd ed). Dubuque, Iowa: Kendall Hunt Publishing Company. pp 143-156.

Northouse, P. G. (2007). *Leadership Theory and Practice*. 4th ed. Thousand Oaks, CA: Sage Publications.

Peters, G. P. (2000). "Is Democracy a Substitute for Ethics?" R. Chapman (Ed.) *Ethics in Public Service for the New Millennium."* Hunts, England, U. K.: Ashgate Publishing, Ltd. P. p.127 – 140.

Rohr, J. A. (1989). *Ethics for Bureaucrats an Essay on Law and Values*. 2nd ed. New York: Marcel Dekker.

Sengova, J.M. (2019). *City of Atlanta Board of Ethics 2018 Annual Report*. Atlanta, Georgia: City of Atlanta Board of Ethics.

Weschler, R. (2013). *Local Government Ethics Programs in a Nutshell*. North Haven, Connecticut: Creative Commons.

OBVIOUS AND NOT SO OBVIOUS UNETHICAL BEHAVIORS AMONG PUBLIC EMPLOYEES

3

INTRODUCTION

It's no secret that unethical behavior exists in all types of organizations. Local governments of course are no exception. This chapter focuses on some of the more frequent misdeeds. Some are very obvious, while others may not be.

It is important to make It clear that unethical behavior in public agencies is not widespread. As this book has suggested in chapter one most public employees are hardworking honest individuals. Indeed, they may be you or your neighbors. Unfortunately, as in real life, even the small number of unethical individuals' behaviors which exist has over time has cost local stakeholders millions of dollars. Even worse, such actions have eroded trust in our governments. Some public officials' unethical behaviors are criminal, while some are much more subtle and are only unethical because they are committed by virtue of one's public actions. Nevertheless, the damage has been done.

OVERT PUBLIC EMPLOYEE UNETHICAL BEHAVIORS: CORRUPTION

When one thinks of forms of governmental officials' unethical behavior, corruption is often the first thought that comes to mind. It is the most overt example of such behavior. Corruption occurs when there is a purposeful breach of public trust and/or abuse of position by public officials, whether elected or appointed. Corrupt individuals ask, demand, solicit, accept or agree to receive anything of value in return for being influenced in the performance of their official duties. (Legal Information Institute, 2024) Corruption is not new. All one has to do as look at the governance of larger American cities from shortly after the Civil War to 1924.

One of the most overt unethical employee behaviors is accepting a kickback or taking a bribe. In this case, the actions are not only unethical, they are illegal. Interestingly, they are also one of the corruptive acts easier to detect. In spite of its overt nature, kickbacks and bribes are still too common.

Modern urban reforms and corruption

Ironically, many of our modern forms of local governments, for example, the city management movement or non-partisan local elections, came as a result the extreme corruption of the urban political machines during that period of time. Wide-spread corruption nurtured the development of the good government reform movement during the Progressive Era. (Neumark, 2023, p.p. 74 – 79; Tindall and Shi, 1996, p. 883)) But It is still questionable how well these reforms have worked. Even after ninety years of urban reforms, unethical behaviors still exist among a very few wayward local government officials. (Note 1)

OTHER FORMS OF OVERT UNETHICAL BEHAVIOR

Time Theft

Over time, because of society constantly evolves, there have been newer forms of unethical behavior. The COVID-19 pandemic has opened the door to one of them which is still ongoing. There has been a substantial uptick in timeclock cheating, or as it is now called "time theft" (Petit, 2024) Time theft has currently become the most frequently exhibited public unethical behavior. As workplaces closed down due to the pandemic and employees went to remote operations, it became substantially easier to report false working times. Ninety-five percent of all organizations have lost revenue due to this practice. (Petit, 2024) Even though many employees consider this to be a minor infraction. Make no mistake, this is theft. Think about all the tax revenue lost due to employee overpayments since this has become a significant issue.

The most common form of remote time theft is "hiding idle time," where employees are able to hide that they are not working by keeping their computer screens on while they may be engaged in non-work activities. (Petit, 2024) It has become the most unethical time theft behavior because this is among the most difficult types of theft to catch.

Hiding idle time is not the only remote working problem. One of the more creative ways of stealing time is something called "buddy punching." (Petit, 2024) Buddy punching is when one employee will cover for another by marking them present either on-line or at the work site, when they are obviously not present during working hours. One finds this in organizations where management is too busy or simply careless about checking who is or who is not actually engaged in doing their work. It could also mean that the supervisor him or herself is cheating the organization. (Note 2) Even though It may be thought as more of a white-collar crime, it is unethical and costs tax-payers millions of dollars over time.

A recent change which may further lead to time theft is who is actually required to report his or her time. Years ago, all employees salaried or not had to indicate the time they arrived and the time they left their place of employment. The clock or the time sheets were right there at the place of employment. Today, with professionals working in a remote environment, salaried employees rarely have to do so. (Taylor, 2019) Some individuals have taken advantage of their newfound privilege.

The electronic-informational revolution may be the impetus for workers going remote, or it may be because of COVID-19. Whatever the reason, our local governments must be on guard to monitor the very few employees engaged in time theft. The accurate monitoring of behavior is an obligation to all of their citizens. Most would agree that taxes are high enough without the added waste of time theft.

Conflict of Interest

One of the most common and ancient lapses of local unethical behavior is when officials in governments become financially beholding to a specific individual or interest group at the expense of a given population. (stakeholders) In this case, a public official has a special relationship with another person or organization and is in a position to financially benefit from that relationship (Weschler, 2012, 26). The term conflict of interest is used for this relationship.

After years of urban government reforms, (Neumark, 2023, p.p. 74-79) conflict of interest is still alive and well and is as insidious as ever. Unfortunately, conflicts of interests are all too common in the workplace. (IntegrityStar, 2016) Conflict occurs when a person's judgement is impaired by acting on behalf of those outside the official public duties at a profit to the employee. (Stark, 2013, p. 173) Those employee puts his or her personal interest above their professional obligations. (Birt, 2023) (Note 3)

Conflict of interest behaviors can be either overt or subtle. Some overt examples of conflict of interest may be when a member of a local board of education who owns a catering company, winds up selling refreshments to that same board to be used at their meetings or caters one of the district's school's activities. Or a county sheriff may also be on the board of directors of a private jail.

Sometimes, the conflict may start innocently. The unethical behavior begins when an employee feels pushed and pulled every which way from all of the outside interests faced at work, including local, state, and/or federal rules and laws; workplace or outside friendships; family problems; financial problems; or even flattery from another individual. (IntegrityStar, 2016) All of these pressures become confusing and sometimes clash with one another. Although the employee may choose to ignore a clash it doesn't always work. Bias then sets in. The requirements of the various interests serve to impair the employee's judgements or actions. In many cases the individuals are not aware of their biases. It becomes easier for the person to concentrate on the few relationships which brings him or her the most benefit without realizing that the persons actions become conflicted and unethical. The individual really needs the money-the individual develops a close relationship with a vendor-family member has a friend who can deliver the service or a good cheaper than if the employee were to follow the government's protocol. Of course, in other cases, a person's conflict of interest is a simple matter of greed.

A conflict of interest may not always be clear. Or it may be quite subtle. For example, participating in writing a grant for a private party who may have a financial interest in the association with the local government (or even as much as helping a client writing the grant), and using government equipment to help out a private client in some way no matter how small that equipment may be (see below), or letting out confidential public information to a private client are all examples of subtle conflicts of interest. (Weschler, 2012, 26).

The following case study brings up a question about a subtle form of conflict of interest. Many citizens outside of government may not be aware why or even that the actions of the Community Development Commission constitute a conflict of intertest. Why is there a question of public ethics? Although fictional, the actions of the parties are based on a real event.

CASE STUDY 3.1: THE NEW BASKETBALL ARENA

This case of a potential conflict of interest concerns a large American city and its community development commission (C.D.C.). The commission is one of several citizen municipal divisions in the executive branch of this city.

Throughout the United States in order to consummate a public or private contract, the party rendering a good or service to another is entitled to a consideration of contract. Both parties must agree on the terms of the contract. (Legal Information Institute 2022) The most common consideration of contract is cash. Cash is preferred because it is unambiguous and easy to trace. In some states any form of payment other than cash is illegal.

For the purpose of this case study it is against this particular city's code of ethics to allow such consideration of contract as free entry (passes or tickets) to an entertainment venue of any nature, or free seats to such an event unless an individual is an actual city representative participant at such an event (Ethics Code A-43, Paragraph 1A).

In 2013 The North American Basketball Association approached this city about the possibility of establishing a major league basketball team. The city had never had any sort of major league sports team. This was a great opportunity to finally become a big-league city. The problem was that it had no suitable arena.

That problem was solved by Gulf and Atlantic Industries, one of the largest industrial concerns in the United States. Under CEO Jill Blankenczeck, the company agreed to put in half of the cost of building an arena. In fact, they were thrilled that the whole country would know the arena as Gulf and Atlantic Arena: clearly the name would be a great boost for their business recognition. The city itself would put in the other half of the building cost.

In order to fund the construction of the arena, the city had to be able to sell bonds. Such bond sales were normally handled by the C.D.C.

for a reasonable handling price. Right from the beginning, the C.D.C. requested a "skybox" (premium seating) as a consideration of contract, which was and is inconsistent with the city's ethic code. The matter reached the attention of the ethics commissioner who turned the matter over to the ethics commission for their review. The commission had final say as to whether or not an ethics complaint would be upheld or not. Indeed, they unanimously approved the commissioner's formal advisory opinion that this particular consideration of contract agreement ran counter to Section A-43-1A of the city's code of ethics.

In early 2019, the C.D.C. came back to the ethics commissioner and eventually to the ethics commission requesting that the board overturn their previous opinion. (As everyone knows, the new request had absolutely nothing to do with the fact that the city would be awarded the All-Star basketball game to be played shortly after the arena would be built.) Once again, the ethics commission refused to allow a skybox as a consideration of contract. Although the C.D.C. threatened to take the members of the commission to court, they realized it was a lost cause.

At this point, the arena was built anyway and the C.D.C. still does not possess their own skybox. The question is, why does the granting of a skybox (or any other variety of premium seating) fall under ethical considerations. Why is the exchange of funds the only ethical way to consummate a contract?

(Neumark 2023, p.p. 197-198)

- Why do you think that using tickets and passes as public considerations of contracts is unethical? (And illegal)
- Would you have known before reading this case study that using tickets and passes as public considerations of contracts are unethical?
- Why do you think that using passes and tickets constitutes a conflict of interest?

Whether or not a conflicts of interest is overt or subtle, they are unethical. To use one's advantage to economic to gain economically is wrong on all accounts. Over the years there had been millions of dollars lost to local taxpayers because of some unscrupulous employee's putting their own economic interests above those of their public employer.

Nepotism

One of the lesser common but overt unethical behaviors found in some local public agencies is nepotism. It can be as overt as actually hiring one's relative or as vague as an employee having the ability to influence the career opportunities for a relative in another department of the municipality. Nepotism can be found among smaller communities where all the citizens know each other, or in larger metropolitan cities. (Note 4)

Why do Americans consider nepotism, particularly nepotism in the public sector, unethical? It goes beyond the American sense of fairness. Since one of the most basic values in American ethics is fairness, nepotism interferes with that belief, as it gives undue advantage to someone who does not necessarily merit this treatment. (Nadler and Schulman, 2006)

Applying nepotism standards can be confusing. Although twenty states have outlawed nepotism, there is disagreement as to what constitutes relationships causing laws in various states to add to this confusion. (Rosenson, 2006, p. 157) In some states, such as Georgia, one is allowed to hire a relative if the position pays less than $10,000. In another state the cutoff is $1,000. In some states relatives beyond the fourth degree of a relationship are allowed. In others it is beyond the second degree. In some states there is no prohibition against nepotism!

Just because there may or may not be a legal prohibition, the ethical question still exists. Whether legal or not, public agencies are constantly in the spotlight. The public is still watching. From a political, if not legal, perspective, the best advice is to stay far away from those actions which can call ones ethical conduct into question.

SUBTLE UNETHICAL PUBLIC EMPLOYEE BEHAVIOR

Using Public Property For Private Use

This takes a quick look at something many of us do. As a member of his city's ethics board, this author was privy to a number of complaints involving the use of the city's property for an employee's private reasons. One of the more egregious actions is when a department manager used the city's vehicle to go to the hairdresser once a week. (during working hours) Sometimes her subordinates would go with her. Needless to say, this manager is no longer an employee of the city. This is obviously an overt ethical behavioral laps. But what about behaviors which the public would consider to be innocent? How often do public employees use their government issued computers or telephone for some private use? This is a very common behavior, especially when one uses the office computer for recreational purposes. What about taking home pens or other small pieces of equipment? We typically look the other way, but that does not erase the fact that using public equipment for one's own use, although admittedly very minor doesn't make it ethical. Where is the cutoff between something very minor and a more significant piece of equipment? The public may not know or even care (probably because they do it themselves), but as a government employee it is important to keep in mind that you are the stewards of all the publicly owned materials and equipment no matter how minor how unimportant they may seem.

Privatization and outsourcing: who runs this town?

The two changes in local governance which have increasingly become popular are privatization and outsourcing. Outsourcing has been around for quite a while. The complete privatization of municipal services is fairly recent.

Whether or not one agrees with Dahl's alienation of control (1982) which posits that the private sector has essentially robbed the public sector of authority, private organizations contractually in charge of local government functions are not necessarily unethical nor are they not in the public interest. Both have become frequent solutions to service provision in local communities. It may be under some circumstances the most efficient way to provide such services.

There are times when the public prefers privatization of local government functions, particularly if they suspect that their elected or appointed officials are not following expected standards of service, behavior, and are not making fair and impartial decisions. With this perception, officials lose their air of legitimacy and as a result lose public support. Whether accurate or not, there is that common belief among some local citizens that the private sector by definition is more ethical and can do a better job. Indeed, some newly incorporated suburban locations have been created as essentially "private cities."

Having private enterprise deliver public service does not present an ethical problem in and of itself. There are, nevertheless, many questions which must be addressed before allowing private entities to act independently of the government in a democratic political system. One of which is at what point does the private entity capture the policy making process without the direct consent of the governed. Others include can a local government recapture the policy making process if it becomes necessary. And what voice in policy development and implementation do the local citizens have when service delivery is instituted by a private organization? Case study 3.2, although fictionalized and exaggerated, presents a real dilemma faced by three real newly incorporated private cities in one particular state. As you read through the case study, keep in mind two questions: How ethical was it for the newly formed government to decide to become a private city, and how ethical were the private service providers?

CASE STUDY 3.2: RED FOX VALLEY THE NEWEST PRIVATE CITY:

The City of Red Fox Valley incorporated out of a very fast-growing suburban township in a midwestern state a few years ago. The three main reasons for the city's choice to separate from the rest of the township were to be able to control their land use, there would be a significant lowering of property tax. Also, incorporation would allow them to form their own police department. They specifically wanted to form their own police force to stop the increasing crime rate in their central city from leaking into their city. After all, no criminal would dare to commit a crime once it became its own city!

Since the residents of the area despised big government, both on the federal as well as the local levels, the charter made it clear that the only employees of the new city would be a part-time mayor, a part-time city council, all of whom would not be paid, and a police department with the minimum number of officers. (All the residents knew that up until now there was no crime in the area, except for some home invasions, a few carjackings and a murder or two.) The remainder of the infrastructure development, recreation, maintenance, finance, water and sewer, and land use policy would be handled by a private corporation or corporations. (Everyone knows that private companies supply services more efficiently, more effectively, and at lower costs.) The charter passed almost unanimously.

The new city thus consummated two contracts: the first was with Independence Fire Protection Company to establish their private fire department. The rest of the municipal services, previously supplied by the township were contracted to the Freedom Municipal Services Corporation.

For the first few years, everything could not go better, The Freedom Municipal Services Corporation built the new city hall building as promised, and the company threw a citywide party for all the residents in the new city park. There were a few minor fits and starts, for example the sanitation workers' strike which piled up trash for a few weeks and a sinkhole which gobbled up the local hardware store. Since they were private concerns, the city had no real say in the labor or infrastructure problems. And anyway, after the three weeks the labor problem was solved, a new hardware store was eventually built and things settled down. The other small issue was being that the Independence Fire Protection Company was not familiar with the streets of the city, they arrived a bit too late to save a burning home. Luckily, no one was hurt, and the homeowner also had insurance.

And she only had to spend two months in a hotel. There were also a few minor glitches with the Freedom Municipal Services Corporation such as water being cut off to some of the wrong customers for nonpayment. And the potholes not being repaired. (Apparently, fixing potholes was accidentally left out of the contract.) A few residents complained that they had a hard time getting a hold of the Freedom Municipal Services Corporation, but that was to be expected since it was a large corporation and customer service had to deal with a much larger group of people from other parts of the country. (The fact that the C.E.O. of Freedom was caught in a very unfortunate compromising position had nothing to do with the quality-of-service delivery.) Other than those minor glitches, the private city worked beautifully.

The real problems came as both contracts expired. The Independence Fire Protection Company increased the dollar amount of the next contract by 40 percent. The company claimed that they needed at least three new firetrucks to serve Red Fox Valley. As the C.E.O. said, trucks only last a few years. What was even more significant, however, was the 75 percent increase requested by Freedom Municipal Services Corporation. According to Freedom, the labor issue cost them a great deal of money. Indeed, due to inflation, everything costs them more.

Now the City of Red Fox Valley was stuck. The city never thought of budgeting for any of the increases demanded by the two private companies. So, they decided to turn to the township to see if they would be willing to service the city. Unfortunately for Red Fox Valley, the township did not have resources to do so. Once the city incorporated, the township had to downsize. The other unfortunate circumstance for the city was that all the other service companies in the country quoted their prices as equal if not more. In the end, the city decided that they had no choice but to go with the same two private companies resulting in a huge local tax increase for the residents. Ironically, the City of Red Fox Valley residents now have the highest property tax in their part of the state, but luckily for them they still have their private city, and they do not have to deal with any unethical public behavior which they still believe automatically comes with local governments.

(Neumark 2023, p.p. 144-145)

- If you were on the original charter commission of the new city of Red Fox Valley, how would you have designed the city's government to be the most ethical and fair possible?
- To what extent do you believe in privatization of municipal services?
- Are there times when you believe that privatization are really necessary and completely ethical?

The Red Fox Valley case study presents a number of important points. One of the definitions of public ethical behavior is that it is unethical for public officials not to do everything possible and equally to their greatest ability for their constituents. Did the mayor and council make the best decisions for the citizens of the city? Were the citizens of Red Fox Valley presented with all sides of the proposal so they could make an informed decision? Could something like this happen in the real world? Are private cities always more ethical than publicly elected and professional managers? Unlike in the Red Fox example, as public officials, it is always important for you to as much as possible make decisions based upon what the future may bring. Neumark calls this crystal balling (Neumark, 2006)

Short of developing a completely private city is outsourcing. Outsourcing is the practice of turning over specific municipal services to providers other than the local government. These may include another local government (intergovernmental agreements), a public district or authority, a public corporation, or a private entity. A few specific examples include the City of Bexley, Ohio obtaining fire services from the City of Columbus, the City of Covington, Kentucky contracting with the Northern Kentucky Water District, The City of New York City receiving recreation services from the New York Parks Authority, and the Jacksonville, Florida Public Schools purchasing transportation services from the First Student Transportation Company.

Even the largest municipalities cannot supply every possible service to their residents. Outsourcing is an excellent, efficient and purely ethical way of supplying what local citizens demand. As with all actions of local governments, municipalities must make sure that turning over a service meets with the highest ethical standards. In the following case study, based on a true incident, unfortunately the city in question did not.

STUDY 3.3: THE CONSOLIDATED WATER COMPANY:

For years, many residents of a major American city had complained about their water service. The quality of the water itself was fine, but the service seemed to be substandard. Water/sewer bills were often inaccurate, the city was slow to fix water leaks in the public right-of-way, and it was difficult to reach the water department by telephone.

The mayor of this city came up with a solution: why not turn water and sewer services over to a private company? The mayor was able to convince the city council that this was in the best interest of the city. It so happened that the mayor had a specific water company in mind: the Consolidated Water Company. The city council agreed to a contract, the water department was dissolved, the equipment was sold, and Consolidated starting serving the municipality with water and sewer services.

However, the service went from bad to worse. Everything the residents had complained about became exaggerated under the private company. Everything that could go wrong, went wrong. Even the purity of the water itself became questionable. In short, the outsourcing policy became a disaster.

With all that was going on with Consolidated, the local newspaper got involved. They started their own investigation. What thy found was that the mayor and the president of the Consolidated Water Company were good friends. Why was this not known to the city council? In addition, it was discovered that the mayor was receiving kickbacks from the company. The findings were turned over to the federal government.

The mayor and executive of the water company were ultimately found guilty of corruption charges and both served time in federal prisons. The city took back, restructured, and changed the name of the department. The department still receives its share of the usual complaints, but at least water leaks get fixed somewhat faster, and the water quality is back to normal.

- What lessons, besides the obvious, can you learn from the above case study?

- If you were a member of the city council what would you have done? What if you were a strong supporter of the mayor up until this point?

What happened in this city is not normal. No one on the city council complained. Unfortunately, it was brought about by indifference. As a public servant, you must be aware of every possible aspect of conflict of interest, even those which are not necessarily overt. The questions that you may have to ask yourself over and over again are, "Is there a chance that my actions may not be completely ethical"? or "What does the local ethics code say about what I decisions I am making"? Remember, conflict of interest may not necessarily be clear and overt.

CONCLUSION

Public employees, as are their private counterparts, are not perfect. We all know this. The purpose of this chapter is not to condemn all of the hard-working local public employees. The point is to make you, the reader and potential or present public official aware of the pitfalls and types of behaviors that are generally deemed unethical. Some are rather obvious; however, some are not. The confusion comes about because certain behaviors which are considered unethical in one community may not be looked upon as wrong in another. We all know that overt conflict of interests, kickbacks, nepotism are clearly unethical. But what about time theft? Have we all been totally honest about how we use company time, especially in an era of remote work? Privatization and outsourcing are not unethical. It is only when we the public employees as well as the citizens of local governments do not take the time to thoroughly educate ourselves over any such proposal that public officials' unethical behavior may creep in.

Those preparing for a career in public service, or those who have just started a position with a local government, may not always be completely aware that he or she is engaged in an unethical behavior, particularly one of the more subtle ones. The purpose of this chapter is not to warn you about illegal behaviors. Undoubtedly, you have been inundated with warnings through your educational process. It is, however, to let you know how such behaviors, especially the less overt types can easily become an embarrassment, or even result in a larger problem, if you are not totally aware of the ramifications of a decision you may make as a public employee.

NOTES

Note 1: Perhaps the most common forms of corruption on the local level are kickback and bribes. One may find kickbacks when a dishonest employee in a procurement department is able to sneak the awarding of a contract to a vendor who is willing to share the profits of the contract under the table to that unethical employee. A bribe is more overt. For example, money is offered to a building inspector who allows a repair to or construction of a building where it would not ordinarily pass code.

Note 2: In this author's several years on an ethics board, he encountered many cases where employees even on the supervisory level who were engaged in various forms of time theft, including using the city's vehicle for personal errands during the time they reported to be in the office working.

Note 3: The financial advantage resulting from a conflict of interest does not necessarily have to be direct. For example, a public employee sneaking company time to work for some outside organization, hoping that eventually he or she will be hired by that organization at a substantially higher pay scale. Or "pulling some strings" from a vendor (giving that vendor an advantage over other suppliers) to hire a friend or relative.

Note 4: Recently, the human resources commissioner for a major American city was suspended and then fired for nepotism. Although this commissioner's daughter was legitimately hired into another position in the city, the daughter wound up having some conflicts with her own supervisor. The commissioner subsequently had the daughter's supervisor fired. Once the local media got ahold of this, the commissioner eventually received the same fate.

CONCEPTS FOR THOUGHT OR RESEARCH

Alienation of control

Bribes

Buddy punching

Corruption

Conflict of interest

Consideration of contract

COVID-19 pandemic

Crystal balling

Hiding idle time

Intergovernmental agreements

Kickbacks

NCSL: National Council of State Legislators

Nepotism

Outsourcing

Pluralism

Political agendas

Political machines

Privatization

Public corporations

Public Districts

Remote working

Tammany Hall

Time theft

Timeclock (timesheet) cheating

Who Governs?

REFERENCES

Birt, J. (2023). "Conflict of Interest: Definition, Examples, and Tips." indeed.com/career-advice/career-development-/conflict-of-interest. Accessed: January 18, 2024.

Dahl R. A. (1982). *Dilemmas of Pluralist Democracy.* New Haven, CT: Yale University Press.

IntegrityStar. (2016). "Understanding Conflict of Interest." Compliance. ucf.edu/understanding-conflict-of-interest/. Accessed: January 18, 2024.

Legal Information Institute (2023). "Definition of Corruption." https://www.law.cornell.edu. Accessed: March 25, 2024.

Nadler, J. and M. Schulman. (2006). "Favoritism, Cronyism, and Nepotism. https://www.scu.Edu/government-ethics/. Accessed: April 6, 2024.

Neumark, G. (2006). Atlanta, Georgia: classroom lectures.

________, G. (2023). *Civic Literacy Politics & Policy in the American City.* Dubuque, IA: Kendall Hunt Publishing Company.

Petit, M. (2024). "Cheating the Time Tracking System: What to do if You Catch Your Employees Doing it. Monatask.com/en/blog/cheating-the-time-tracking-system-what-to-do-If-you-catch-your-employees-doing-it. Accessed: February 1, 2024.

Rosenson, A. (2006) "The Effects of Legislative Law: An Institutional Perspective." In D. Saint-Martin and F Thompson (e Jaids). *Public Ethics and Governance: Standards and Practices in Comparative Perspective* (Volume 14). Amsterdam, Netherlands: Elsevier Jai.

Stark, A. 2013. "Conflict of Interest in Politics and Psychology." Frederickson, H. G. and R. K. Ghere (Eds). *Ethics in Public Management* (2 ed). Armonk, New York: M. E, Sharp. 172 - 192.

Taylor, J. C., Jr. (2019). "My Employees May be Fabricating Work Hours on Their Timesheet.

What Should I Do? Ask HR." usatoday.com/story/money/careers/career-advice/2019/01/29/timesheet-cheater-how-deal-employee-fabricating-work-hours/2656368002. Accessed: February 1, 2024.

Weschler, R. (2013). *Local Government Ethics Programs in a Nutshell.* North Haven, Connecticut: Creative Commons.

PUBLIC LEADERSHIP AND EMPLOYEE ETHICS: A CLOSER LOOK

INTRODUCTION

This chapter looks at the connection between public leadership and employees with ethics. We all want our public leaders to be moral and able. Clearly, these are high sounding attributes to be admired. Can a person not have these qualities and still be a great leader? As you read through this chapter think about your own personal attributes and how you can be a better and the most ethical public decision maker. There is no question, but that a leader has a fundamental role in determining how ethical his or her employees will be.

Leadership is a term which seems to be tossed around a great deal. For the purpose of this chapter, leadership is defined as those empowered to make decisions for a given population. Ethical leadership is those who make the right decision for an entire population and not just for oneself (Heifetz, 1994, p. 113). As you read through this chapter ask yourself what do the local public expect from their government leaders as well as employees. These expectations, however, sometimes lead to confusion and conflict.

LEADERSHIP

One cannot emphasize the importance of leadership in making sure that our local governments function within the highest level of ethical behavior. This is the case whether the leadership is elected or professionally appointed. The extent that an organization turns out to be completely ethical falls on the shoulders of those who manage our public agencies. It is the ability of leadership that sets one workplace apart from others (Berrios, 2023). An organization's leadership can foster the best or worst employee conduct. (Note 1)

The challenges of local leadership

Being a leader whether in the public, nonprofit, or private sectors can at times be difficult. There are many challenges especially for those in charge of our local governments. One of them is the public demand that their government officials must show exceptional leadership in the face of any difficult situation. A principal characteristic of a healthy ethics environment is how well the community trusts its public leadership. It is greatly facilitated by leaders who believe that citizens' trust in government is of paramount to importance. In order to gain that level of trust, good leaders encourage the open discussion every matter possible. (Weschler, 2013, p. 23). (Note 2) To the extent that a leader puts the community before himself or herself is what serves to tie one in authority to ethical conduct. In the face of all of the political pressure on a local official that individual must use his or her ability to make the correct decision for the entire community. An ethical leader is able to use his or her ability and authority to mobilize people to face tough issues. What makes leadership even more important in a difficult situation is that such decision makers are faced with proximate choices and limited, often conflicting, information. There is not a simple linear decision path from a consensus on ultimate values and goals when things go wrong (Jones, 1997, p. 228).

Beyond garnering trust in an emergency, the ethical leader provides an environment in which there is nurturance and empathy" (Heifetz, 1994, 113). Important decisions lie in the everyday shaping of policy, not merely in the heroic stand at the time of crisis (Kaplan, 1963, p. 103).

Leaders and personal ethics

One's personal integrity serves as a guide, perhaps the only guide, among all of the possible crises and everyday choices. He or she is able to set the tone to blend the public's sense of morality with that of their government. Whether tough or easy political choices, the personal ethics of that policy maker is one of the most important factors in making such choices. It is a responsibility that comes with public office (Kaplan, 1963, p. 103). For example, in the face of an impending emergency situation where the population faces a mandatory evacuation, does the ethical leader evacuate with his or her family or stay behind to direct emergency personnel? In a municipal budgetary crisis, does the leadership cut his or her salary?

The following are some of the more important personal ethical traits of ethical leaders:

- Respect for others
- Serving others
- Just and fair
- Honest
- The ability to build community and develop a sense of belonging to his or he
- Employees
- Leads by example
- Displays integrity
- Accepts accountability when things go wrong
- Shows empathy
- Driven by personal values
- Aware of implicit fairness
- Isn't afraid of open communication
- Transparent actions
- Constantly trying to understand how their decisions impact the public
- Zero tolerance for ethical violations
- Willingness to evolve
- Looks into the future (Note 3),
- Not afraid of admitting mistakes,
- Takes Employee's complaints seriously as possible "red flags."

(Lewis, 2023, 5; Ethico, 2023)

All organizations, whether public or private, have their own culture. (Note 4) Some of the more important characteristics of one's work culture includes how well the employees get along with each other, To what extent employees are willing to go beyond the minimum of expectations, how pleased employees are with the working conditions, how the members of the organization communicate with one another, how approachable is the leader, a sense of whether or not leadership cares, and indeed how ethical is the operation of the organization. (Cote, 2023; Berrios, 2023) In most organizations the shape of the culture comes from the top. It is not just a matter of the leader performing his or her obligations, leadership sets the tone of the entire operation, which has a direct effect on its output whether private or public.

EMPLOYEES

There are 23.7 million public employees at all levels of government in the United States. (Congress Reports, 2022) Adding in the 3.8 million public school educators (National Center for Education Statistics, 2022), the total comes to 27.5 million public employees, or about nine percent of all Americans. The percentage is even higher when one considers not the entire population but only the 207 millions of adult Americans. (Zippia, 2023) The percentage of those working in the public sector comes to about 13 percent of all Americans eligible to work including all of the public officials who serve in elected, professional, or appointed positions as well as those in the front-line positions. Afterall, the public is most likely to come into contact with those individuals who are on the front lines. Public employees constitute a significant number of individuals working for various governments.

Who are public employees? Are they different than their private sector counterparts? Are they you?

Right from the outset, there are some factors which separate public employees from private employees is a covenant with the public to ensure that they will promote the public interest without favoritism or discrimination (Pelissero, 2021). The public should expect nothing less. This is especially true of the close contact Americans have with local government employees. (Newman, 2016, p. 2) and having fewer employees it is easier for the public to keep track of their activities. As a result, local employees are often under closer scrutiny by citizen awareness as well as in the media. Local government employees are often kept on a straighter path than the more remote state and federal employees. In smaller cities in particular, the local employees are well known to the residents.

Private sector employees

The public may also expect ethical behavior from private employees but does not hold private employees accountable in the same way in which professional local government employees are. With a strong commitment to capitalism and the rights of private enterprises to operate as they wish, unless there is a fragrant violation of American sensibilities, most individuals are more tolerant of the behavior of private employees. They may boycott a particular product if they are really unhappy about the ethical behavior of a high-level private company's conduct, but there are other companies to which to turn as a substitute. The choice of other governments is obviously not so easy.

Most Americans consider poor corporate employee behavior as none of their business as long as such behavior does not personally affect them. In addition what behaviors take place in American private organizations is often done under the veil of secrecy.

Receiving personal Gifts

Receiving gifts from vendors may be frowned upon in private business organizations but is especially strictly prohibited in the public sector. For example, under no circumstances is an employee of the City of Atlanta's government allowed to accept a gift or gratuity (City of Atlanta, Georgia Ethics Code Sec. 2-811 and 2817). This also holds true for non-paid employees such as board and commission members. If it came to light that a private corporate employee received baseball game tickets, a gift over $10 in value, a kick-back from some vendor, or free travel in a vendor's corporate jet, would either the public or the media treat that violation in the same way as if it happened in a government organization? The employee may receive a reprimand, but would most Americans really care? Would most Americans even know?

Case study 4.1 presents a fictional account based upon a real incident. The result of this employee receiving certain gifts speaks for itself.

CASE STUDY 4.1: RECEIVING GIFTS

It came to light to the ethics commissioner in a large American city that a certain motor pool supervisor was receiving major league baseball tickets on a regular basis from a prohibited source against the city's written code of ethics. (Note 5)

The motor pool division is an essential part of the city's government. Besides managing the use of city vehicles, it is responsible for purchasing public vehicles as well as parts to be used as needed. A specific vendor was chosen by the city council to supply the parts through the competitive bidding process.

Aaron Partain was a motor pool supervisor. In one year, he was found to have accepted eleven baseball tickets from that vendor. Although the tickets were not normally solicited by Mr. Partain, in one occasion, he actually used his official city email to request one. He also received three entertainment tickets from other vendors. It was further discovered that Mr. Partain solicited future tickets from a variety of vendors doing business with the city.

An anonymous whistle blower finally filed a complaint to the city's ethics commissioner. After a thorough investigation, Mr. Partain was terminated, the incident was placed in his personnel file, and he was charged a $6,000 fine. Local governments take private gifts to public personnel very seriously. It is a rare government that simply looks the other way when this sort of unethical behavior takes place.

- Would the result of Mr. Partain's taking the gratuities be the same if it were to happen in a private organization? You be the judge.

Perception

A stark difference between employees in the two sectors relates to the public's perception. In the years of teaching public employees' ethical behavior as a part of his subject material, this author has found that the majority of students automatically perceive that a public employee is going to be unethical. The higher the position, the more likely this perception comes into play. Although there may never be any proof presented, beyond a shadow of a doubt that government employees are any better or worse than any other individual in the private sector workplace, many of us assume this is the case. Public officials are not a different species of humans! They are not 'bloodless bureaucrats. They are the people at the heart of government (Ingraham, 2005, 283). And yet, this is the way so many of us view our public servants.

There are, of course, ethical shortcomings of some individuals working in the public sector. Such behavior cannot be acceptable. When a public employee's misconduct comes to light, it further advances this false perception. Perhaps, the two most common reasons why the perception exists are that they are much more in the public spotlight, and they are directly responsible for the use of the constituents tax monies. (Note 6)

Employee ethical requirements

No matter what the perception may be, the reality is that most governments care very much about ethical conduct. Following is a list of expected public employees' behavior on all levels of government. (Note 7)

- Public service is a public trust, requiring employees to place loyalty to the Constitution(s), the laws, and ethical principles above private gain.
- Employees shall not hold financial interests that conflict with the conscientious of duty.

- Employees shall not engage in financial transactions using nonpublic government information or allow improper use of such information to further any private interest.
- An employ shall not, except pursuant to such reasonable expectations as are provided by regulation, solicit, or accept any gift or either item of monetary value from any person or entity seeking official action from, doing business with, or conducting activities regulated by the employee's agency, or whose interests may be substantially affected by the performance or nonperformance of the employee's duties.
- Employees shall put forth honest effort in the performance of their duties.
- Employees shall make no unauthorized commitments or promises of any kind purporting to bind the government.
- Employees shall not use public office for private gain.
- Employees shall act impartially and not give preferential treatment to any private organization or individual.
- Employees shall protect and conserve [public] property and shall not use it for other than authorized activities.
- Employees shall not engage in outside employment or activities, including seeking or negotiating for employment, that conflict with official government duties and responsibilities.
- Employees shall disclose waste, fraud, abuse, and corruption or appropriate authorities.
- Employees shall satisfy in good faith their obligations as citizens, including all just financial obligations, especially those such as federal, state, or local taxes that are imposed by law.
- Employees shall adhere to all laws and regulation that provide equal opportunity for all Americans regardless of race, color, religion, sex (Note 6), national origin, age, or handicap.
- Employees shall endeavor to avoid any actions creating the appearance that they are violating the law or ethical standards promulgated pursuant to this order.

Source: National Institutes of Health NIH Ethics Program

A new reality, working remotely

Remote working appears here to stay. Although public employees were among the first to be called back to work as the pandemic of 2019 started to wane, many of them are still allowed to continue working remotely.

Many workers find remote work to be a positive experience. Berrios(2023) found that the overall respondent to a survey was that he or she loves the flexibility of working from home as it has greatly enhanced the person's work/life balance. Remote working has become quite desirable. Public organizations, however, must be aware of the ethical pitfalls of this new environment, including a lack of productivity, a lack of effective managerial controls, and a concern about confidentiality, including cybersecurity. (Kittner, 2020)

There are ways to make remote working effective and productive. The following suggests ten rules to combat possible ethical problems between managers and their employees or employees to other employees in a remote working environment. (Miller, 2020) They all point to how to communicate effectively with all others as you would in a face-to-face working environment.

- Show the same respect to your employees and or coworkers as you would in the in-person environment.
- Be honest and punctual about the time spent while engaged in your remote work.
- Be sincere.
- Take advantage of video calls such as Zoom or Skype.
- Strive to produce High-quality work.
- Have frequent and meaningful one-on-one conferences.
- Be self-motivated.
- Maintain an all-inclusive positive workplace culture.
- Keep a proper work-life balance.

Based on Madeline Miller's 10 Ethical Rules to Remember About Remote Work (2020)

Fortunately, most employees follow these rules regularly. (Berrios 2023)

SHARED ETHICAL RESPONSIBILITY: PUBLIC EMPLOYEES, CITIZENS (PUBLIC CORPORATE STAKEHOLDERS)

Employees as shareholders

Many public employees understand that they have a role as shareholders in their organizations and are important resources in identifying those who make unethical choices. In a recent survey of public employees, integrity was found to be more important than pay. (Thornberry, 2019)   To that end, whistleblower protection laws have increasingly been established and enforced.

Not only do all employees have the obligation to foster high ethical standards in their workplace, but they also have more ability in doing so than one may think, although sometimes public officials may not be aware of their own power.

The most common way may not necessarily through being a whistleblower, although that very often happens. It is through the increasing use of their organizations' evaluation sites. (Snell, 2017, p. 6) Rating sites can serve as a "red flag" to potential ethical misconduct. Upper public management, such as commissioners and city council members have to take these sites seriously. They allow all levels of employees to let those in policymaking positions know exactly what may be brewing. To the extent that the upper-level managers will listen to those concerns, (If they don't, the voters will) the remainder of the workers can have a great deal of power to make positive changes. As workplace evaluations continue to become increasingly more common, they work side by side with elections which serve the very same function.

Citizens as shareholders

Not only public employees but their constituents share the responsibility with the ethical delivery of government services. All are a part of shared governance. Many local residents are members of boards, commissions, elected positions, **and voters.**

If one considers the structure of an incorporated local political unit as similar to the structure of a private corporation. (In some states such as Ohio, they are called corporations.) in a real sense, we, the public, are the shareholders of our local governments just as the shareholders are in a private corporation. *Incorporated* local governments are public corporations. The similarities are amazing: the mayor is the CEO, the city council is the board of directors, and we, the citizens, are the shareholders. As with any stockholder, we must take on the responsibility of keeping the corporation financed and operating within the highest level of ethical standards. It is our shared responsibility. Although the general population may not have a hand in choosing a career or politically appointed official, it is up to the public to know all about candidates for local government jobs. It is our responsibility to let government officials know when we are not satisfied with the behavior from a public employee. **We are also the government.** The most obvious way of making sure that the most ethical individuals are employed by our local government is through the electoral process: although indirect, taking the time to really know the candidates is an essential step. After all, in the end, it is our elected officials who are responsible for hiring government employees, especially managers, who in turn often have the responsibility of hiring the best workers. let our officials know who the "bad apples" are.

Most local governments already partner with numerous boards and commissions. Why not create a citizen's HR advisory board? Let those on this board work hand-in-hand with the HR department. It follows that if an individual is interested enough in becoming a member of such a board, that individual would certainly have an interest in public ethics.

When citizens as well as public employees have the shared responsibility within the local governmental structure in insuring the best and most ethical employees possible, it becomes one more important tool in making sure that our local governments continue to operate within the highest level of ethics possible. Americans already share responsibility for ethical behavior among private organizations by switching products or services. Shared responsibility also holds true in the public sector. Consumers of government services must pay as much attention to what happens in the public sector as they do with private goods in the marketplace.

CONCLUSION

Chapter four takes on an in-depth look at public organizations from two sides: leadership and employees. Both have their challenges as well as ethical requirements.

The greatest challenge of those in the leadership roles of local public organizations is the ability to garner trust among the public stakeholders. Those governments' whose citizens view as highly ethical and can meet challenges as they arise are the ones who will be the most successful in gaining that trust.

The ability to garner trust applies to public employees as well. The important thing to remember about our local government employees is that they are people as you or I. They may be you neighbors, friends, relatives, or even you. They certainly are not some sort of bloodless machine. Of course, there are always going to be bad actors. If there weren't, governments wouldn't need ethics codes.

There appears to be an on-going ideal that public employees are less ethical than their private counterparts, without any evidence whatsoever that this is the case. Why does this myth continue to exist? For one, those who work for public agencies are covered much more closely by various media outlets than those employees in the private sector. This may be the case because governments are the keepers of public monies, (the guardians of our taxes). Another reason is that stories about wrongdoing in our governments draw in more readership or viewers. We also may interact more with public employees, especially on the local level, than with those in the private sector: our educators, local license bureaus, city councils, or county commissioners, police, or fire personnel, even mayors and city managers to name a few.

As we know, myths themselves lead to skewed perception. The irony is that government employees are often held more accountable by their employer to a higher standard of ethical behavior than in the private sector.

Public officials as well as individuals share governing. Since this is particularly true on the local level, because of its close proximity to the people. It is to the benefit of local citizens to participate actively in their municipal governance. Informed voting is one way. Being a member of a local board or commission is another. All of us live in a local government, and it is our responsibility to make sure that it functions with the highest ethical standards. The good news is that there are several lists of ethical standards available to our governments as well as the citizens. This chapter has included the list published by the National Institutes of Health. Government employees and the public should have no difficulty knowing what is expected.

NOTES

Note 1: Chapter Four outlines the differences between private and public ethical expectations. Although from time to time it mentions the private sector, except for working without a bottom line, and being under the media microscope, leadership and working in the public sector is not always so different than that in private organizations. This is not to exclude required public obligations.

Note 2: For many individuals, public trust appears to be more important than trust in some private organizations. This may be because it is much easier to switch from one private goods and service provider to another when something unsatisfactory happens than it is to pick up and relocate in another community "voting with one's feet." (Tiebout 1956)

Note 3: This applies to all levels of public management who have the autonomy to make important decisions.

Note 4: The concept of public organizations and their culture will be taken up in depth in the next chapter.

Note 5: A prohibited source is defined as any individual or organization doing business or wishing to do business with a public agency: accepting any sort of gift from a prohibited source is always *prima facia* unethical.

Note 6: Private employees are also responsible for the use of the public's money. Unlike governments, how their funds are used is more indirect. Afterall, when private organizations charge for a good or service, they must take into account losses which may occur,

CONCEPTS FOR THOUGHT OR RESEARCH

Accountability

Citizens as shareholders

Citizen boards and commissions

Ethical Behavior

Ethical leadership

Ethics Codes

Ethical rules for remote working.

Future consequences of present decisions (crystal balling)

General-purpose governments

Gifts or gratuities

Honesty

Integrity

Leadership

Leadership attributes

Local government employees

Media coverage of local employees

Morality

National Institutes of Health Ethics Program

Organizational evaluation sites

Outsourcing

Percentage of working adults

Perception

Private sector

Prohibited source

Public corporations

Public employee covenant

Public managers

Public-private government services

Private sector

Rating sites

Remote working honesty and productivity

Respect

Shared governance

Single purpose governments

Transparency

Trust in government

Trust in leadership

Voting with one's feet (Public Choice Economics)

REFERENCES

Berrios, Laura. (2023) "Survey Results: Workplace Integrity More Important Than Pay." Atlanta Journal Constitution. Ajc.com. Accessed: August 11, 2023.

City of Atlanta, Georgia Code of Ethics. (2023) http: www.AtlantaGa.gov. Accessed November 18, 2023.

Congress Reports. (2022). https://www.congress.gov>117th-congress. Accessed: November 10, 2023.

Cote, C. (2023). "How Does Leadership Influence Organizational Culture?." https://oneline.hbs.edu/blog/post/organizationsl-culture-and-leadership. Accessed: November 24, 2023.

Ethico. (2023). "12 Characteristics of an Ethical Leader to Adopt Today." https://Ethico.com. Accessed: November 19, 2023.

Galveston History Center. (nd). www.galvestonhistorycenter.org/research/1900-storm. Accessed: September 12, 2024.

Heifetz, R. A. (1994). *Leadership Without Easy Answers.* Cambridge, MA: Harvard University Press

Ingraham, P. W. (2005). "The Federal Public Service: The People and the Challenge." In J. D Aberbach and M. A. Peterson (Eds). *The Executive Branch.* Oxford, U. K.: Oxford University Press. P.p. 283 – 311.

Jones, M. D. (2012). "The City Governs." In *R. Steinbacher & V. O. Benson* (Eds.). *Introduction to Urban Studies* (4th ed.). Dubuque, IA. Kendall Hunt Publishing Company.

Kaplan, A. (1963). *American Ethics and Public Policy.* New York: Oxford University Press.

Kittner, E. P. (2020). "The Ethics of Remote Work." *Insight*, winter 2020. https://icpas.org. Accessed: November 12, 2023.

Lewis, N. S. (2023). "Can Ethical Leadership be Successful in the New Hybrid Work Environment?" *Ethics in Action* 19. P.p. 5-6.

Miller, M. (2020). "10 Ethical Rules to Remember About Remote Work." https://hrcsuite.com. Accessed: November 12, 2023.

National Center for Education Statistics. (2022). https://nces.ed.gov. Accessed: November 10, 2023

National Institutes of Health. (2023). https://oir.nih.gov. Accessed: October 11, 2023.

Neumark, G. (2023). *Civic Literacy Politics and Policy in the American City.* Dubuque, Iowa: Kendall Hunt Publishing Company.

Newman, H. K. (2016). "Citizenship in the Local Community" G. Neumark (Ed). *Citizenship in The Local Community* (3rd ed). Dubuque, Iowa: Kendall Hunt Publishing Company. P.p. 143-156.

Pellissero, J. P. (2021). www.scu.edu/government-ethics/resources/what-is-government/ethics/civility/conflict/of/interest/in/government/. Accessed: September 5, 2023.

Snell, R. (2017) "Study: Employee Rating Sites can Red Flag Potential Misconduct. "*Compliance & Ethics Professional.* R. Snell (ed). 14, 7. P.6)

Thornberry, T. (2019). Jackson, Mississippi. Unpublished written communication with the Author.

Tiebout, C. (1956). "A Pure Theory of Local Expenditures." *Journal of Political Economy* (64, 5). P.p. 416 – 424.

Weshler, R. (2013). *Local Government Ethics Reform Programs in a Nutshell.* New Haven, Connecticut: Creative Commons

Zippia. (2023). https://zippia.com. Accessed: November 11, 2023.

PUBLIC ORGANIZATIONAL CULTURE, AND ETHICAL BEHAVIOR

INTRODUCTION

Neither leadership nor public employees operate in a vacuum. The actual culture of an organization has a great deal to say about how employees react with the public, one another, and leadership. The culture of our government organizations is dictated by the people who work there. In a democratic nation, people have choices. Both employees as well as leadership can choose to "take the high road" or to cut ethical corners as they feel are needed. The focus on the ethical practices of public organizations whether strong or weak does not mean that individuals themselves working for that organization, have no moral responsibility (Hoekveld and Needham, 2013, p. 1639) no matter what the culture may be. The focus of this chapter is on the interrelationship between culture, public organizations, and ethical behavior.

ETHOS

Most organizations, including the public, have what is called "bureaucratic ethos." (Pugh, 1991, p. 10) **Ethos** refers to the guiding principles as to how a person, organization, or a community should operate. Ethos determines what is important and how they plan to operate. This includes guiding beliefs, aspirations, and its moral commitment to the public. To that end, many government agencies have published mission statements. One can say that an organization's ethos guides it ethics.

Since in practice some do not necessarily follow their own philosophy, ethos from ethics is not the same. Some government organizations have wonderfully sounding mission statements but in reality operate in a cloud of secrecy and questionable ethical behaviors. These behaviors then become engrained into their culture.

CULTURE

Culture is defined as the sum total of knowledge, experience, beliefs, values, attitudes, interpretation of meanings, priorities, religion, personal roles, modes of communication, acceptable social interaction, the types of clothes and hats one normally wears, and the use of symbols. (Texas A & M, 2023) It is a pattern of shared basic concepts about how to succeed and align actions accordingly." (Priest, 2017, p. 23). We normally attribute it to groups. It may not necessarily formalized, although some aspects of culture could include such strong beliefs that they become legitimized into actual law.

Thus, organizations have their culture. The specifics may vary, but the definition remains the same as other types of culture be it national, regional, undefined group, ethnic, or local. There is a strong and direct connection between ethical behavior and an organization's culture: "Employees figure out what it takes for them to succeed and align their actions accordingly, subconsciously as well as consciously." Formal communications, training, procedures, and systems may make a difference; however, less formal subtle messages often sent by colleagues and leaders influence the perception of culture even more. (Priest, 2017, p. 23) Many of the aspects of culture can be directly related to public organizations.

PUBLIC ORGANIZATIONS AND CULTURE

The various cultures found in public organizations are not a great deal different than those in the private sector. There are some differences, however. One pertains to the lack of a bottom line. If the culture in a public agency makes ethical behavior a top priority, for example, it is not to sell a product to the public to make a profit. It's much more about the obligation of public service to a community. Even if some employees of public organizations display questionable ethical conduct, it is more often likely for individual advancement through the ranks or just a lack of caring. Another is those, particularly in the top echelons of public agencies who take advantage of their position to use tax money for their own purposes, obviously an individual failing not connected to the governmental culture. (Unless it is the culture of the public agency to turn the other head. See Case Study 5.1)

Another difference is the effect of unethical private behavior, completely outside of his or her position in the public organization. Such behaviors can have a negative impact on the overall functioning of that agency, especially if the public organization is known for priding themselves on their culture of public service. The publicity surrounding these behaviors may cause other employees and the public to lose confidence in their mission. (Note 1)

Not all public organizations have the same quality of ethical control over their employees. A pattern of unethical actions can be tied to poor internal controls. Providing an open and safe line of communication is crucial for an organization to ensure that all ethical expectations are being upheld.

It does not take long for an employee to pick up the culture for better or worse, whether the highest level of ethical behavior is always expected or not. This does not mean that individuals have no choice. We all know the difference between right and wrong. A question that surfaces in public organizations is do subordinates carry out the orders of a supervisor in the face of serious concerns regarding that order? If the subordinates do what is asked of them, and if such action is questionable, who is acting unethically in this case? If the subordinate refuses to carry out an order which he or she considers unethical, what happens to his or her job? How does the public react when such circumstances come to light? Do we accept such behavior? The case study below paints a picture of subordinates actually facing such an ethical dilemma in a local government.

CASE STUDY 5.1: THE ATLANTA PUBLIC SCHOOLS' CHEATING SCANDAL

From 2009 until 2013, the Atlanta Public Schools District faced one of the most infamous cheating scandals in the history of education in the United States. Forty-four out of fifty-six schools were found to be cheating on state required test scores. (Georgia Public Policy Foundation, 2015) Although the Atlanta superintendent of schools did not survive cancer to have her case heard in a court of law, it was alleged that she, and some of her immediate subordinates, ordered principals and teachers to conspire to change test scores by erasing answers and putting in their own in some of the lower performing schools on the pain of the educators losing their jobs. Thirty-eight principals along with several upper-level administrators in the central office, and the superintendent herself were charged. (Procter and Lupiani, 2024)

Should these individuals have followed the chain of command, or should they have taken the ethical route and refused to cheat on these tests? Better test scores would lead to much additional funding needed for the students and perhaps to better educational performance. Historical test performance in some Atlanta Public Schools was so low that better results were out of the question. The problem for the front lines educators was, if that educator refused, he or she often the sole provider of the family, could lose his or her job. Harvard University education professor Michael Koretz calls this "applied anxiety" (Koretz, 2018, p. 27).

Several educators in this case were presented with an ethical decision. Did they have a choice in this matter? Some educators made the ethical choice while there were those facing this dilemma took an unethical road: changing the incorrect answers on required standardized tests. (Some of these educators actually made it into a fun activity by having test changing parties at their homes. This attitude clearly was consistent with the culture of the Atlanta Public Schools at the time.)

The cheating on tests went on until the local then national press made it all public. Ultimately, the educators did lose their jobs. Some were accessed fines and even received jail time, and all who were found to be guilty lost their certification to teach in the state of Georgia.

It may have been easy to tell these educators to follow the ethical route without regard to the personal consequences. Or was it?

By now the culture of the Atlanta Public Schools has drastically changed for the better. Their system has had two very professional educators as the superintendents whose mission was to change the culture. Also, it is very important that in spite of the previous culture, most of the educators went to work and did their job consistently with the high standards parents of the system expect.

The above discussion is based on "Learning to Cheat." By J. Brian Charles in Governing magazine, September 2018.

The Atlanta Public School's cheating scandal brings a relevant questions to you the reader as present or future public servants. How you would react in similar circumstances:

- If you were a teacher in one of the schools caught cheating, you were your family's only breadwinner, and you were put under pressure by your administrators, what choice would you have made?
- How does this incident relate to the culture of one or more of the organization in which you may be a member?
- Would you be a whistleblower?
- It was assumed that the superintendent supported the cheating in order to bring in more funds to a cash strapped school system. Do the ends justify the means?
- In the end, who was cheated? Why? If you are or were an employee of a public agency, who would be cheated if a similar situation arose in your workplace?

- Have you actually ever been in a similar situation? If so, what choice did you make?

The above case points out the kind culture of dilemma that an individual may face during the course of a public service career. Culture, ethics and politics are sometimes at odds. There is not always an easy answer to this dilemma. (Note 2)

Public organizations may not always be perfect, but the vast majority of them operate within a positive culture of service to the public.

The role of culture clash in ethical policy making

Important as it is, for a public employee to know the organization's culture, it is equally essential for the individual to be aware of culture clash. Culture clash occurs when one culture is unable to mesh with another especially within the same geographic area. It is normally due to lack of understanding. It may be found in all variants of culture including in public agencies. Sometimes the manifestations of these culture clashes are more subtle, while other times they seem like open warfare. It results from varied groups develop differing versions of ethics, values, and customs. In other words, culture clash means "us and them." (Neumark, 2011) Culture clashes can be found on many levels ranging from subcultures, within organizations, to national, to international cultures. (Kottak, 2011, p. 38) Beyond simply being us and them, each culture sometimes explicitly blinds its adherents to those of another. (Douglas and Wildavsky, 1982, p.175).

Cultural clash is not planned, it is not part of the ethos of any of the parties involved, nor is it logical. It comes from a refusal to accept the different beliefs, including what is ethical, from others.

Case Study 5.2 brings out an example of a public agency's culture clash with the community because of a difference in its academic paradigm. Both parties believe their point of view is the most ethical, representing the absolute good of their communities. It is to the extent that their actions may self-serving manner that an ethical question arises.

CASE STUDY 5.2: THE ATLANTA BELTLINE: PUBLIC ADMINISTRATION AND PLURALIST POLITICS, A CULTURAL CLASH—THE CASE OF TENTH AND MONROE

The Atlanta BeltLine project is the largest public infrastructure development in the history of the state of Georgia if not the entire country. The Atlanta BeltLine, is a 22-mile loop of light-rail transit, walking trails, and parks. (Neumark, 2012, p. 3). It promises to transform the entire city, if not all of the Atlanta metropolitan area. Since its inception, in late 2005, it is probably the most talked-about construction project in the city and state. Millions of dollars and thousands of man hours have been poured into its development. Starting as a rails to trails project, it has mushroomed every kind of private urban development one can imagine, including residential, commercial, entertainment, recreation, and offices. Many of these are contained in massive high-rise buildings.

Progress on the implementation of the Atlanta BeltLine stopped cold for two years due to a the open animosity between the local community and the BeltLine developers, The Atlanta BeltLine, Incorporated (ABI), a branch of the Atlanta Development Authority. The animosity can be explained by a culture clash between a well-educated upper-middle class community and a very professional public agency. The root of the clash can be found in the different views regarding two different academic disciplines.

From one perspective ABI seemed to ignore many political considerations, particularly those emanating from the neighborhoods. From the Neighborhoods' point of view ABI was acting unethically because they refused to serve the community's needs. From another point of view, ABI was doing exactly what they are supposed to do, and their behavior was completely ethical. They were serving the best interests of the entire city.

The culture clash came to a head over how to develop a small piece of land at Tenth and Monroe in northeast Atlanta. It came very close to being scrapped. It actually came to a halt for two years.

The piece of land in question was acquired by ABI in the purchase of railroad right-of-way, necessary to continue the BeltLine. The actual piece itself was not needed but had to be included in the entire purchase.

The disagreement was between ABI and a loose coalition of several neighborhoods surrounding this unremarkable piece of land. In 2006, a suburban developer was ready to purchase the land and prepared to construct two forty-story condominium towers on the property. This land use was vigorously opposed by three neighboring communities, who after the two-year stalemate were successful in convincing the city not to rezone the property.

This conflict was not only a significant success for neighborhood interests, but also served to strengthen the political influence of the local neighborhoods in regard to all BeltLine policy development. In the end, the planning department realized that the rezoning would not be in the best interest of the city as a whole.

ABI's policy was to have the property rezoned to a higher density and sell it. Higher density would bring in a greater return on their investment and help to fund further BeltLine development. It would also bring in more traffic in an area where the residents believe there is already too much.

There was an additional issue which exacerbated this conflict. Several residential properties adjacent to the property had been purchased by another developer who had stated publicly that he is planning to consolidate and redevelop the houses on these properties for a more intensive use. ABI was in support of offering these properties to that developer, making their property even more valuable.

The neighborhoods saw the BeltLine's plan for higher density as a way of destroying their single-family way of life, while ABI saw this as a financial opportunity which would benefit the entire city. With their increasing political power, the neighborhoods were willing and able to stop the entire BeltLine process to keep their neighborhoods intact. Eventually, neighborhoods from all over the city joined the fray and let ABI know that they would not support any additional taxes needed to continue with the BeltLine.

This standoff, although political, was not a territorial power grab. It went much deeper. It came about as a result of the cultural clash between two very different political cultures: the planning professionals and public administration paradigm on one hand and traditional pluralistic political science on the other. Historically, both have very little comprehension and appreciation of the other.

If one were to observe the actions of the neighborhood residents, they were very much consistent with the pluralist political predictions (Note 4) (Note 5). Planners and public administrators take a much more rational perspective of governing. Both opposing paradigms have their own cultures.

Public administration and its culture: We argue that public administration as a discipline can be considered to have its own culture. "Cultures exist when traditions and customs are transmitted through learning." (Kottak, 2011, p.14) This is the case with public administrators. (Note 6)

Most public administrators and managers through their professional educational process understand that conflict and politics cannot be completely avoided. Although the idea that they can be separated is still a significant part of their professional education and informs much of their culture. They understand that policy decisions may not be popular, but they constitute the best possible outcomes *in their professional opinions*. This vision of apolitical policy making is still contained within the public management culture over one hundred years later. (Ostrom, 1974, p. 26).

Currently, there is still little communication between the two disciplines even within the university setting. There also appears to be no movement toward any sort of consolidation. The message that is implied in the separation of disciplines is clear: there remains a normative belief in the dichotomy among public administrative and managerial practitioners.

Another important aspect of the public administration culture related to the down paying of political considerations is more of an emphasis on global concerns. One can see this in the present case. The more global concern is with the entire city of Atlanta not any specific neighborhood(s). Policy should be applied for the good of an entire population regardless of what dissent or political issues may come into play. Although this view is necessary in developing and executing a city-wide policy, at the same time, it tends to render public administrators less capable of dealing with neighborhood politics.

Similarly, another element of the cultural outlook of the discipline is the public administration's belief that the ordinary citizen is either not interested or perhaps not even capable of understanding the nuances of complex policy issues. Most local citizens are neither experts nor professionals. Public ideas emanating from the community are simply not as important since such ideas come from untrained individuals. (Reich, 1988, p. 3)

Although in the case of Tenth and Monroe, both the planning department as well as ABI were required to solicit citizen input, in the end, it was the input of the professional administrators who made the important decisions. (Note 7)

This was the culture of Atlanta BeltLine, Inc. They had a very different outlook than pluralist political science regarding Tenth and Monroe. To those public administrators who are tasked with making the best decision for the entire city, it was perfectly ethical to downplay the desires of the neighborhoods. From their cultural point of view, it was perfectly acceptable to pursue high density development of Tenth and Monroe for the highest and best use and good for the city.

Pluralist Political Science and Its Culture: Pluralist political science as a discipline has a very different culture. If one were to summarize the essence of pluralist political science in a single word, that word may very well be *conflict*. It is the positive driving force behind politics. Every component of the discipline, including the study of power relationships, flows from the understanding of conflict at all levels. Both conflict and politics are important and positive components of American public life. (Note 8)

"Conflict is the greatest positive motivator in the political process." (Presthus, 1980, p. 72) Conflict goes hand-in-hand with liberty: "To condemn all political conflict is to condemn diversity and liberty as evils." (Dahl, 1998, p. 150) More to the point in this case study, conflict is an especially important component of urban development.

Urban development is all about conflicting interests, contested plans and policy choices. (Logan and Molotch, 2007, p. viii)

From the culture of traditional pluralist political science, conflict is at the very heart of all policy development. Without it there is no need for policy and no need for *governance*. Svara. (2002, 214) It is the very essence of what Lasswell (1936) meant when he wrote his classic study *Politics: Who Gets What, When, and How*. Clearly the neighborhoods had no problem dealing with conflict. After all, they were able to hold up the entire process for two years.

The other important element of pluralist political science, of course, is "pluralism." Conflict is only half the picture. The political process must be open to all. Pluralist political scientists understand that any final decision must be made by government officials, but the real role of government is that of a referee. (Dahl 1961) At the same time, it is the public which plays a major role in informing government decisions. (Note 9)

Openness, democracy, and inclusiveness are all important factors in the culture of pluralist political science. Decisions may not be the best policy, but they are the best decisions possible in an open democracy. (Thomas, 1975) (Note 10)

Finally, the geographical scope of pluralist political science is more limited compared to the scope of public administration. The concern is generally in the immediate area where a particular conflict is taking place.

Comparing the two cultures: 10th and Monroe

One can easily observe a fundamental difference between the two disciplines concerning the development of 10th and Monroe. One of the first difference concerns their view of the geographical scope of ABI's perspective. ABI takes a much wider view. Their ethical responsibility is city wide. Denser development benefits the entire city of Atlanta. One neighborhood is not more important than another.

The neighborhoods following the more traditional pluralist political science view more locally oriented: what specifically affects them. In the case of the BeltLine, their neighborhoods come out as the most important. They are ethically bound to protect their immediate interests. Their cultural orientation is consistent with the tug and pull concept of pluralist political science: policy, although imperfect, comes about from all of the interested parties pulling against each other. In this case the neighborhoods with their local interests pulling against ABI with their city-wide interest.

Atlanta BeltLine, Inc's. takes an apolitical, scientific approach while avoiding conflict. It is their fundamental cultural belief that their policies are in the best interest of the entire city. There decisions should reflect the separation of policy and politics. They are ethically bound to uphold the interests of the entire city of Atlanta.

Culture Clash:

The disagreement between the community and Atlanta Beltline, Inc. is a bona fide example of a cultural clash. Such a clash can occur between two academic paradigms. Cultural class occurs when two or more cultures disagree about their beliefs, ethics, values, or ways of life. (Fielding, 2012, p.1) Both disciplines represent most of the factors that define culture, and there is clearly a significant disagreement as to how each side sees the world. At the point where the progress on the BeltLine was stopped, neither were willing to budge.

It would appear that no neighborhood thought had been given to the effects of the possible decision to stop the BeltLine on the forty-three

other BeltLine neighborhoods located in all of quadrants throughout the remainder of the city. Their interest in determining who gets
what, where, when, why, and how applied only to their one little corner of Atlanta.

This tug-of-war went on for two years. Finally on March 20, 2012,
Rukiya Eaddy, the former external affairs manager for the Atlanta Belt-
Line, Inc., announced that the Atlanta City Council had agreed to ap-
prove the BeltLine master plan, excluding higher density zoning for the
corner of Tenth and Monroe. The project could now go forward.

How and why did this ABI about-face happen? According to the local
councilmember, Alex Wan, it appears that the ABI completely capit-
ulated to the demands of the neighborhood. They realized that to get
the neighborhood to agree to any higher density use for their Tenth
and Monroe property was an uphill battle. The entire project was
much too important to lose. After the protracted fight, ABI wanted
the project to move forward again.

Does the settlement mean that the neighborhoods and ABI have
shown a significant willingness to understand each other's point of
view? Were each willing to take the ethical high road to break the im-
passe? As long as the culture clash remains, however, there is going
to be future stalemates regarding the BeltLine. As of the present time,
the property remains an empty parking lot for a nearby restaurant,
although ABI is collecting the revenue by charging a fee for parking.

This entire affair adds evidence of the lack of understanding that the
BeltLine staffers have had on the political culture of many of the Atlanta
neighborhoods. Had they understood Atlanta neighborhood politics,
this would have been settled much more easily without a two-year delay.
In the end ABI gained nothing but an empty parking lot. Perhaps from
this incident, the managers will understand that there is a difference between their background and the political culture of the city of Atlanta.

The neighborhoods also must understand why the BeltLine leadership believes it is perfectly ethical to try to sell off excess property

to the "highest and best use" proposals. Afterall, the administrators
are entrusted to make the best economic decisions for the City of
Atlanta. The real problem was, and perhaps still is, because of their
cultural clash the inability to understand each other's ethical behavior: should a neighborhood or should the entire city be protected.
Neither the neighborhoods or ABI displayed the highest standard of
ethical policy making. Understanding the nature of the culture clash
and its relationship to ethics can allow both cultures to work together
to ensure a successful BeltLine project. (Note 11)

Based upon G. Neumark (2012)

Understanding culture clash is important for public organizations. Although it seems obvious when two very different cultures are geographically close some sort of clash will ensue, it is much less obvious that it
happens within public organizations, or as written above two different paradigms within employees of the same organization. In some cases culture
clash among subcultures can be just as powerful. Along with the clash
comes differences in ethical priorities. As a public official, you must be
aware of these differences to ensure the greatest functioning of your public
organization.

THE CULTURAL ETHICAL DILEMMAS: PUBLIC ORGANIZATIONS IN A DEMOCRACY

Americans believe that public organizations should be open. democratic,
and ethical. This is at the very core and survival of democracy. (Thompson,
2020). These expectations, however, bring up a dilemma. Openness and
ethical behavior may not or cannot always be compatible. There are times
within the most open democracy when a public agency may not or cannot
always follow the most ethical and moral political decisions. Government
administrators on all levels are faced with this paradox: Overriding attention to purely moral concerns might amount to a neglect of the admin-

istrator's institutional obligations. (Burke 1986). In other words, public officials may sometimes be more obligated to the political process (which is a very real and important aspect of carrying out the work entrusted to the organization) and not necessarily to the moral code of the organization itself. Balancing the organization's mission with the surrounding political concerns can put a public servant in the position of having to make a choice between what is considered morally correct or some unethical behavior behind the scenes in order to make sure that the organization accomplishes its objectives. It is the old adage do the ends justify the means? (Rohr, 2013, p. 60) Sometimes not being open is a matter of public safety and security. Should a chief of police let the public know every fact of an investigation, including who may be working undercover? Does the FBI publish a list of its informants? What if that informant is publicly known to be an unethical individual? The cultural aspect of this dilemma can also present a problem. Some public organization can become so used to operating in secrecy, needed or not, which becomes ingrained in the organizational culture. Unethical behavior may become a necessary tool under some circumstances, but it must be used judiciously before it becomes another aspect of a public organization's culture.

There are opposing views. opposing view. (Denhardt, 1989, p. 187) She is quite clear in addressing this paradox: political activity by a [public official] can be justified only 'in the pursuit of democratic ideas (1989, p. 187). There is never a justification for public employee unethical behavior. Unethical behavior in an anathema to democratic standards. This sort of behavior can turn out to be a "slippery slope."

CONCLUSION

To say that individuals in public organizations act according to their actual government's expectations is not always the case. The ethos is one thing. Organizational culture is another which often presents a strong determinant as to how public employees really behave. There is a close interrelated connection among culture, public organizations, and ethical behavior.

Differing cultures are found in entire societies. Culture, the sum total of knowledge, experience, beliefs, values, attitudes, interpretation of meanings, priorities, religion, personal roles, modes of communication, acceptable social interaction, the use of symbols (Texas A & M, 2023), can be found in all organizations, including governments.

Look at the cultures of the various organizations to which you belong. Such a close look can bring you to the understanding that your social or workplace culture dominates its stated purposes and decisions.

Although not radically different than one would find in the private sector, there are some cultural differences between private and public organizations. Perhaps, the most important is the direct responsibility to the public. This aspect of culture is found in most public agencies. The best of our government organizations understands their mission and go about their business with a high regard for personnel ethical conduct. The fact is that many public agencies are under a microscope, from the communities in which they serve and from the media. Their every move is often watched and dissected in the media, putting a certain amount of the stress on one's public life. (In some cases, even in their private life.) This also has an effect on the culture.

Sometimes cultures in close proximity clash. We think of cultural clash as misunderstanding and animosity between two societies, but it also occurs between organizations and even academic disciplines as in the case of Tenth and Monroe presented above.

Finally, this chapter points out that public organizations are not perfect. A significant number of public employees can sometimes engage in largescale unethical ethical behavior because of their cultural outlook. The Atlanta school cheating scandal presents such a case.

It is most important point of this chapter is for public employees to understand the relationship between various types of culture and their own views on ethical behavior. This understanding can lead to a much more successful public service career.

NOTES

Note 1: An example of where a public official's private behavior made a significant impact on the organization's ability to carry out its mission is the publicity surrounding the prosecution of a former president in Fulton County, Georgia.

Note 2: On the other hand, a Kentucky hotel general manager lauds the culture of the governments of the City of Covington and Kenton County. She suggests to this author that their culture of public service leads them to be efficient and do the utmost to be of service to the residents and businesses alike (Wusterfeld, 2024).

Note 3: To say that both paradigms have very little appreciation for the other is not an overstatement. Public administration may have started out as a subfield of political science, but during the age of American Scientific Rationalism, such advocates as Woodrow Wilson pushed for it to become a separate discipline. The idea was to take politics out of governing and make it more scientific. This concept has been carried into the present time. In many universities the two disciplines are administered in separate colleges if not in separate departments.

Note 4: The plural form, points, is used here because although similar there a number of nuanced pluralist models.

Note 5: Our argument is not that the neighborhood is comprised of pluralist political scientists, but as with most educated upper-middle class Americans, these citizens have been enculturated to view the American political system as essentially pluralist. The predominant view is that government is and should be run by the people, and if people disagree with its actions, they have every right to address these wrongs in any legal and peaceful means possible. They may accept that professionals may have an important role in governance, but professionals can be wrong and may not take every possible factor into consideration in the policy making process.

Note 6: What this case study is referring to is how and what is being taught in most public administration curriculum, leading to the modern ethos of public administration as a discipline. The same argument can be made about political science.

Note 7: As required by both local and federal policy and law, the BeltLine administrators held meeting after meeting throughout the entire city. The meetings consisted of discussions, question and answers, lectures, and charettes. In the end, however, the real decisions regarding the BeltLine were made by ABI, not the local citizens.

Note 8: This is true only to a point. Both power and politics are positive as long as they do not get out of hand.

Note 9: Findings show that ordinary citizens, given the correct information and time for discussion are very capable of understanding complex and sometimes technical issues and reaching pertinent conclusions about significant public matters. (Fung and Wright, 2012, p. 9)

Note 10: Private citizens would not put forth the effort to settle a conflict if they believed that their desired results were impossible to achieve. Many Americans still believe that communities have the ability to affect public policy. Nothing will change if citizens don't participate in the political process. This belief is ingrained in the culture of traditional American political science.

Note 11: For a classic in-depth study of how the culture of different public organizations with differing paradigms affected a very important national public policy decision, see Graham Allison's *Essence of Decision Explaining the Cuban Missile Crisis* (1971). What role did the ethical outlook of each paradigm outlined by Allison play in their potential decision regarding the Cuban Missile Crisis?

CONCEPTS FOR THOUGHT OR RESEARCH

Atlanta Public Schools' Cheating
Scandal

Atlanta BeltLine

Atlanta BeltLine, Inc.

Bureaucratic ethos

Conflict

Culture

Culture clash

Cultural norms

Democracy

Dichotomy

Ethical dilemmas

Ethos

Highest and best use

Neighborhoods

Organizational culture

Paradigms

Public administration

Public organizations in a democracy

Scientific Management

Who gets, what, where, when, why,
and how

Who governs?

Woodrow Wilson

REFERENCES

Burke, J. P. (1986). *Bureaucratic Responsibility*. Baltimore, MD: Johns Hopkins University Press.

Charles, J. B. (2018). "Learning to Cheat." *Governing* Magazine (September 2018 ed.). 25-30.

Dahl, R. A. (1961). *Who Governs?* New Haven, CT: Yale University Press.

__________ (1998). *Democracy in the United States: Promise and Performance*. 3rd ed. Chicago: Rand McNally College Publishing Company.

Denhardt, K. G. (1989). "The Management of Ideas: A Political Perspective of Ethics." *Public Administrative Review*, 49. P. p. 187 – 193.

Douglas, M. and A. Wildavsky. (1982). *Risk and Culture*. Berkeley: University of California Press.

Fielding, R. (2012). "Culture Clash." Looprevil Press. http://looprevilpress.org/2012/06/28/culture-clash/. Accessed March 3, 2013.

Fung, A. and E. O. Wright. (2012). Quoted in Carole Pateman. "Participatory Democracy Revisited." *American Political Science Review* 10 (1). 7–19.

Georgia Public Policy Foundation. (2015). "The Atlanta Public Schools Cheating Scandal." https://www.georgiapolicy.org/news/the-atlanta-public-schools-cheating-scandal/ Accessed: August 14, 2024.

Hoekveld, G. and B. Needham. (2013). "Planning Practices Between Ethics and the Power Game Making and Applying an Ethics Code for Planning Agencies." *International Journal Of Urban and Regional Research*, 37 (5). p.p. 1638-1653.

Koretz, M. (2018). Quoted in J. Brian Charles. "Learning to Cheat." *Governing* Magazine (September 2018 ed.). 25-30.

Kottak, C. P. (2011). *Anthropology Appreciating Human Diversity* 14th ed. New York: Mc Graw Hill.

Logan, J. R., and H. L. Molotch. (2007). *Urban Fortunes: The Political Economy of Place*, 20th anniversary ed. Berkeley: University of California Press.

Neumark, G. (2006). Atlanta, GA: classroom lectures.

_________ G. (2011). Atlanta, GA: classroom lectures.

_______ G. (2012). "The Atlanta BeltLine: Public Administration and Politics, a Cultural Clash—the Case of Tenth and Monroe" *Proceedings of the Georgia Political Science Association.* p.p. 3 – 20.

Newman, H. K. (2010). "Citizenship in the Local Community." In *Citizenship, the Community, and Public Service*, ed. Harvey K. Newman. Dubuque, IA: Kendall Hunt Publishing Company, 1–7.

Ostrom, V. (1974). *The Intellectual Crisis in American Public Administration.* Tuscaloosa, Alabama: University of Alabama Press.

Pateman, Carole. 2012. "Participatory Democracy Revisited." *American Political Science Review* 10 (1): 7–19.

Presthus, Robert. 1980. "Towards a Post-Pluralist Theory of Democratic Stability." In *Three Faces of Pluralism: Political, Ethnic, and Religious*, ed. Stanislaw Ehrlich and Graham Wootton. West Meade, Farnborough, Hants, UK: Gower Publishing Company, Ltd., 65–79.

Priest, S. (2017). "Strengthening a Culture of Integrity." *Compliance & Ethics Professional.* February 2017. 23.

Procter, A and J. Lupiani. 2024. "Atlanta Public Schools Cheating Scandal: Remaining Defendants Make Deal to Avoid Prison." https://fox5atlanta.com/news/atlanta-Public-schools-cheating-scandal-defendants-court. Accessed: August 14, 2024.

Pugh, D. L. (1991). "The Origins of Ethical Frameworks in Public Administration." J. S. Bowman (Ed). *Ethical Frontiers in Public Management Seeking New Strategies for Resolving Ethical Dilemmas."* San Francisco: Jossey-Bass Publishers. p.p. 9 – 33.

Reich, R. B. (1988). "Introduction" in *The power of Public Ideas.* R. B. Reich (ed). Cambridge, MA: Harvard University Press.

Rohr, J. A. (1989). *Ethics for Bureaucrats an Essay on Law and Values* (2nd ed.). New York: Marcel Dekker.

Svara, J. H. (2002). "City Council Roles, Performance, and the Form of Government." In *The Future of Local Government Administration: The Hansell Symposium,* ed. T. N. Clark and J. Nalbandian. Washington, DC: ICMA, 214.

Texas A & M. (2023) https://peopletamu.edu. Accessed: January 20, 2024.

Thomas, W. (1975) Atlanta, GA: classroom lectures.

Thompson, J. L. (2020). "Ethics are Integral to our Democracy." https://www.therepublic.com/2020/09/17/

Wusterfeld, B. (2024) Covington, Kentucky. Written communication with the author.

INTRODDUCTION

Capturing the Policy Making Process: Who Runs This Town?

In the world of "hyperpluralism," (Sometimes spelled as two words) polarization, and political pressure the question arises: who runs this town. (longly, 2021) There are so many public and private groups and organizations pulling every which way that it seems as if government and policy making is out of control. This chapter takes up this question and its implications for public ethical behavior.

POLITICS IN AMERICA: TRADITIONAL POLITICAL PLURALISM, NEO-PLURALISM, AND INCREMENTALISM

To understand why there is so much pressure on our modern public officials it will be helpful to look at some of the American policy development models. Understanding these may help to clarify your thoughts as to how decisions are made and the importance of ethics.

Traditional political pluralism

Our country operates under a system of democratic political pluralism. Even with all its variants and imperfections, traditional political pluralism is still the most common model of policy making. Pluralism had its roots long before it became an American political philosophy. It emerged with ancient Greek philosophers. (Norman, nd, p.1)

Its modern American roots are found in David Truman's conception of group theory. (Truman, 1951, p.p. 505-515) Robert Dahl, in his classic work *Who Governs?* (1961) set the stage for the traditional American pluralist model.

In its simplest descriptive form pluralism suggests that in a political democracy there are many organizations each with their own political agendas. (Note 1) Organizations are most likely to participate only when some sort of political disturbance arises. When a policy issue does come up that affects the organization they do what they can to either have that policy approved or denied. They then become part of an issue network. (Heclo, 1995, p.p. 262-287) (Note 2) When there is opposition to a proposed policy, a tug and pull of multiple organizations, some in favor, some against, begins. Organizations often form coalitions with other organizations for additional support. Coalitions are fluid and usually break apart once the issue has been decided.

In the pluralist model, the role of government is that of referee. It takes all of the various arguments into consideration and comes up with the best possible policy, which may not necessarily be the best policy.

One of the most important beliefs of pluralism is that any individual can become a part of the political process through membership in organizations. Because most individuals belong to multiple organizations, political power becomes dispersed and balanced: the policy goals of one of an individual's organization may conflict with the goals of another of that person's organizations. This constant conflict of organizational wishes tends to moderate the tugs and pulls.

Neo-pluralism

In recent years, newer variants of American pluralism have surfaced as critiques of how the theory actually works. One which has gained traction is "neo-pluralism." (McFarland, 2004) Foremost in the critique of traditional pluralism is the idea that political power and policy outcomes are in some sort of balance. Neo-pluralists posit that some organizations, individuals, and groups clearly have more political power and influence than others. Also, not every entity is able to form coalitions. They also believe that the political process does not involve organizations only. Groups of all kinds, including ad-hoc groups as well as individuals have an important role in determining policy outcomes. They believe that traditional American political pluralism is unrealistic. It does a poor job of describing how important policy decisions are made in today's political environment. They sound the alarm on the breakdown of the American policy development system causing, not only political imbalance but a high degree of the causation of some officials to make unethical decisions under pressures.

Incrementalism: the science of muddling through

Another of the well-known dissents to American pluralism is the notion of incrementalism, or government simply "muddling through." (Lindblom, 1950, p.p. 79-88) According to this model, governments have little to no input from the public, including interest groups. Governments make their decisions on their own volition, ignoring more of the outside pressure than the other political models. Policy decisions are made on a public agency's assumption of a need. They may not be the best and most ethical decisions, however. The case study below presents such a situation.

CASE STUDY 6.1: RAIL OR BUS?

In November 2017, residents of the city of Atlanta voted in favor of a one percent sales tax to provide improved public transportation to underserved neighborhoods in all parts of the city. The selling point was for the development of light rail.

By 2021, the Metropolitan Atlanta Rapid Transit Authority (MARTA) made the decision to use Bus Rapid Transit (BRT) instead, a much newer and cost-effective technology to service these neighborhoods. These "Buses" would run mostly on their own right-of-way and would serve the neighborhoods just as efficiently as rail.

The decision was clearly incremental. There was very little public input. Once the decision was made solely by MARTA, there was a significant outcry from the communities where light rail had been promised. Residents all over the city complained about broken promises. Although there was a lot of unhappiness with the decision, city-wide organized opposition never developed, and MARTA stood firm. The BRT system is now being constructed in two of the neighborhoods.

- Was it ethical for MARTA to tell the voters one thing but then change their mind after the voters approved a specific plan of action? Or is it important to be flexible as conditions change?
- Would MARTA's decision have been more ethical if all of the interested parties would have participated in an issue network?

INTEREST GROUPS

Perhaps the greatest source of political pressure comes from interest groups. (Note 3) These groups and organizations continue to put pressure on our governments to walk a fine line. (Which they sometimes fall off!)

The United States is a nation of free public/private cooperation. From the very beginning of our nation a public/private economy has always been accepted as the best and only economic solution for the maintenance and growth of our economy. One result of the American system has produced a nation of private organizations on all levels, many of which have been established for the sole purpose of influencing government decisions: Organization is a means to power . . . Americans enjoy the fundamental right to influence government (Dye and Sparrow, 2009, p. 289).

There is nothing unethical about the formation and existence of these interest groups. It is only when members of a group choose to put undue pressure of governments does the question of ethical behavior come into play: How public employees react to this pressure, ethically or not.

Interest groups are not monolithic, and they can form for any number of purposes. For example institutional interest groups whose members support a particular institute ranging from a school to a specific company, or to a non-profit organization. Labor groups are formed to protect the rights of workers. Public interest groups are the watchdogs of the political process. Economic interest groups are there to protect a specific industry. (Birkland, 2011, p.p. 160-161) Also interest groups attempt to gain strength from forming form coalitions. (Mc Farland, 2004, p. 161) Once their goal is achieved the coalition often breaks apart and can become oppositional with each other.

Added to coalitions are the issue networks which include not only those in favor of a specific policy, but also the opposition. (Heclo, 1995). Both those in favor of a policy as well as those opposed can form their own coalitions. The important point is that everyone is free to participate in the policy process.

The problem with some interest groups

As long as public employees stay neutral the American public/private economic and policy system is consistent with how a democratic representative is supposed to work. In some cases, however, interest groups attempt to take over a government's policy making function. One finds this on all levels of government from national to local. As a result, the interest group system is frequently attacked because it can obstruct the majority from implementing its preference in public policy. (Dye and Sparrow, 2009, p. 289). None of this negates a government's responsibility to make its well-informed ethical decisions.

In our free society, it is the goal of an interest group is to obtain the most beneficial policy decisions. However, they also have the responsibility of making decisions which should be of benefit to all of society. There must be a balance, but with so many interest groups this does not always happen.

Public/private interest group partnerships

There are circumstances when a private organization becomes responsible for the establishment and implementation of public policy, such as in privatization or outsourcing. That does not take away from the government's responsibility of making sure that policy is made in a fair, equitable, and ethical manner. It is also the obligation of private citizens to be vigilant and aware of any form of ethical concerns resulting from these partnerships.

Interest groups and you

Interest groups are not some isolated entities. In reality, interest groups are you. How many organizations do you belong to at this moment: Your college? Your workplace? Your professional organization(s) Any myriad of social clubs? Your neighborhood? (If you are a homeowner, you are more likely to participate in your local government than if you are a renter.) (Incerti, 2024, p.1604) Sometimes your organizations are in complete agreement over political issues, but sometimes they are at odds. The support that you and other members give to a group will help to determine your group's involvement in the political process.

Your membership in interest groups brings up the theme running through this entire book: responsibility and vigilance. The majority of interest groups are fair and ethical and operate with responsibility. It is only when the interest group system strays from this responsibility that it may affect ethical behaviors among public officials.

TOO MANY COOKS: HYPERPLURALISM

The greatest problem among American political participation is the sheer numbers of interest groups. This is known as hyperpluralism. Our country is in an era of political hyperpluralism. It exists when multiple groups, individuals, or organizations become so numerous and politically strong that the government is unable to function effectively. (Longly, 2021, p. 1) Hyperpluralism exists on all government levels, including the local and all have a significant impact on the behavior of public officials.

The concern is how it can cause unethical behavior easily to creep into decisions made by our public servants. The pressure on public employees who have to make decisions in the presence of uncountable interest groups can manifest itself in two overt unethical choices. First, the decision maker may find him or herself biased in favor of one or more of the interest groups simply by expedience. That can happen of course in a normal pluralist political environment, but it is more likely when the share number of groups seems out of control. The other choice is to make a rash decision which in the long run may not be the most ethical choice: too much input can make for poor decisions.

Many, if not most, interest groups in our country are related to business interests. In our local economies, governments need business leadership to effectively govern. Many are unable alone to mobilize the resources needed to do so, so they turn to various interest groups. (Phillips, 2010, p. 497) In theory, there should be a partnership. The ethical problem appears when this partnership gets out of hand and the local governments lose control of the "partners."

Impacts of hyperpluralism:

- Benefiting specific groups or organizations at the expense of the general population,
- Government policymakers folding under pressure and making rash, or even unethical decisions,
- Legislative gridlock,
- Slowing or preventing altogether important legislation,
- Uneven distribution of socioeconomic power,
- Undermining the precepts of democracy,
- Limiting political power.

(Longley, 2021, p.p. 5-6)

Interest group politics did not start out being hyperpluralistic. There have always been groups and organizations wanting something from the government. And they have always applied pressure on public officials to that end. However, as our society became more technological and sophisticated more and more groups emerged. As an outgrowth of the development of interest group politics political observers believe that there are just too many organizations constantly trying to influence government decisions. One may think of hyperpluralism as pluralism on steroids causing political decisions to become out of the control. It has now become the rule rather than the exception as government leadership continues to lose the ability to account for all of the difficult and competing private interests. Their shortcut decisions may relieve the public employees of the political stress often at the expense of making decisions that are right for all of the citizens. (Dahl, 1983)

The fictional case study below shows a rather extreme case of hyperpluralism and the difficulty it presents in establishing a straightforward policy. As you read through this case, see if you can pick up any other instances of questionable ethical public behavior.

CASE STUDY 6.2: THE WALL

Snow City, a small mostly agricultural city on the banks of the Big River in Bovine County in the northeastern section of a state in the northern United States is the home to the Bovine Feed Corporation, the largest livestock feed processor in the country; Northview University; as well as a very highly recognized city run public-school system, the Snowbird Inn, the states most well-known hotel and fine dining resort; and a thriving central business district.

The city has a problem: every year, as late spring approaches and the snows start to melt and causes the river to overflow its banks on occasion, it seeps into the Bovine factory, along with the Big River City Park, and portions of the university. Roy Richmann, the CEO of the Bovine Feed Corporation, was obviously not very happy with these floods. He claims that they have cost him millions of dollars on ruined products and lost production. Finally, he decided to go directly to Mayor Richard Plowfield and have him do something to stop the flooding. He was especially unhappy with Mayor Plowfield since Richmann was one of the mayor's greatest political supporters and largest campaign contributor. He is also a member of the six-member city council.

During lunch at his country club, to which he invited Mayor Plow-field, he approached the mayor with his solution. His idea was to build a large retaining wall between the river and his plant. The wall would also be extended to the municipal park and the university campus, all located on the next properties from the factory.

To no one's surprise, the mayor ordered the public works commissioner, George Wurkmann, to draw up a concrete plan for a retaining wall. The total cost of such a wall came in at $5,586,098.37, including the actual cement wall, labor, as well as having to buy out ten riverside homes, through eminent domain, to obtain all of the needed property.

Since Richmann as well as Sarah Dean, the university president, were both on the city council, the mayor already had two votes for the project. He was sure the third vote would come from Councilmember Sarah Plowfield, his second cousin president of the First Northeast State National Bank.

Although the bank was happy to help finance a portion of the wall, the city needed a way to finance the remainder, so they contacted the local finance expert, Morton Richmann. They could not use bonds since they had already reached their bonding limit, and the state would not allow them to form a single purpose wall authority. Then the mayor and Richmann came up with the idea. Why not export the tax? Just establish a twenty-five percent hotel and restaurant tax. With all of the powerful backing, it became quite obvious that the wall would be built.

Once the project was announced the mayor started receiving telephone calls, emails, texts, and letters. The first call came from his cousin. The bank was immediately ready to loan him $1,500,000, with only a 35 percent interest rate. The bank's board was elated, especially for the loan's 35 percent. The city was even willing to lower that bank's property tax by 30 percent. The city council was extremely happy to get Richmann off their backs. They were all in! University

President Dean couldn't possibly be happier. The wall would also serve to solve their flooding problem. Then there was the building trades union. What a wonderful solution to the city's unemployment problem. Putting the unemployed construction workers to work building the wall was a brilliant idea. The owner of the local concrete factory and union president, Brett Wurkmann, lent his full support to the project. The All-American Heritage Society gave its strongest endorsement to the project. The wall would stop the flood of illegal immigrants coming across from Canada. (At least two were caught in the previous two years*) I. M. Prezmen, the local newspaper editor firmly supported the project. He wrote an editorial as soon as the proposal was released to the public claiming how important it was to keep the feed factory in the city. If the wall were not built and the flooding continued, the company would surely move out. The Parks Commissioner, Wanda Forrest-Dean, was extremely pleased that her park would no longer flood every spring. Finally, Bovine County was very happy since this would be a city project, and they did not have to put in a dime.

The obvious, however, did not necessarily go as planned. What the mayor did not count on were all of the dissenters. Within one hour of the announcement, a very upset school board president, Reed Schuller, called the mayor. He just found out that because of having to build the retaining wall, there would be no money in the next budget for a badly needed new elementary school. The city would be using what surplus it had for the wall. The chamber of commerce was livid! How dare the city add an extra tax to the city's main cash cow, the Snowbird inn? The manager of the Inn had already received three cancellations from individuals who had heard about the new tax from the newspaper editorial within the first hour of the announcement. Rose Busch, the Big City Park Conservatory president saw the retaining wall as disaster. It would take away from the natural beauty of the park. The park conservatory even threatened to call Governor Koldsen about the proposal. The Snow City Central Business District Association was very concerned since the inn was the biggest draw in the city. They flat out said they could not support the project. The state's Environment Board also voiced their lack of support for the project. The beautiful Big River did not need a wall. Nothing should spoil the beauty of the river. In addition, the ten property owners whose properties were in danger formed the Big River Homeowners Association to fight the proposal. The mayor also received a call from the angry Canadian Consul saying the city was discriminating against Canadian citizens. Finally, the EPA was about to launch a study to see if the city, even the authority had to build a wall.

The next two weeks were dreadful for the mayor. He kept on receiving constant messages from both the supporters as well as the detractors. The stress was so bad, he could not sleep. The residents of Snow City were inexorably divided on the project. The Riverview Neighborhood Association loved the idea. The Southtown Neighborhood association hated it. You can be sure that the mayor heard from both of the neighborhood associations. It seemed that everyone loved it or hated the idea. Everything seemed so out of control. Finally, he could no longer stand the stress. He needed an easy way out, so he called a special meeting of the city council to vote on the issue once and for all. As expected, the vote was three for and three against. Mayor Plowfield was allowed to vote to break the tie and immediately signed the retaining wall ordinance into law.

Within twenty-fours, three of the organizations opposed to the wall filed suit in the State Superior Court. The Snow City Board of Education, the Snow City Central Business District, and the Big River Homeowners Association, based their argument on the premise that such a wall could possibly cause irreparable damage to the future and economy of the city as well as damage to the immediate environment. The city feed company countered sued claiming that the wall was necessary, and that the floods presented a crisis.

That was two years ago. The suit and counter suits are still tied up in court. The wall is going nowhere, and Snow City is as polarized as ever, each claiming the other side acted completely unethically. Although he was reelected by three votes, no one knows where the mayor is.

*It was discovered somewhat later that the first illegal immigrant, was not an immigrant at all. He was fishing and the current in the Big River forced him ashore by accident

(Neumark 2023, p.p. 200-201)

Although the case study is complete fantasy, there is a serious side to the point. It doesn't matter if such a breach of public ethical behavior probably could never happen, it is the same type of dilemma faced by any mayor. It is not unreasonable to assume that policy makers face this sort of hyperpluralism dilemma on a regular basis. Well-meaning public officials can wind up with questionable behavior. Most would agree that the mayor's actions were unethical. But why? Was it unethical to listen to an important private citizen? Was the idea of building a wall unethical from the beginning? Or was it unethical for the mayor to go ahead and push through the ordinance, just to get it over with? Had there been fewer organizations interfering with the decision would the mayor and city council have acted more ethically? Since so many different political agendas came into play, were the politics in and of itself unethical? If you were in the same dilemma, what would you do?

Alienation of control: Who runs this town?

The Wall represents not only hyperpluralism but also alienation of control. Dahl presented this concern and warning about the development of hyperpluralism affecting the implementation of public policy in his classic book *Who Governs?* (1961). He used the term "alienation of control," the turning over of what should be the function of government to private entities to express his concern. (Dahl, 1983, p.p. 23-34). It is one thing for a government to have to deal with so many groups and organizations and be able to adjust and balance policy development. It is quite another to turn over the policy making process to these groups and organizations. He questioned the ethical conduct of a government when it allows private organizations to put any traditional function of a democratic government beyond the public control and placed into the hands of nongovernment elites.

Governments turning certain functions to private enterprise such as out-sourcing is not in question as long as the public has access to the orga-nizations performing the functions either directly or through the public officials. Think about who influences policy decisions in your local com-munity. Who runs your town?

THE GROWTH MACHINE: A POTENTIAL FOR UNETHICAL POLICY MAKING

Hyperpluralism is not the only danger regarding pressure put on public ethical behavior. Particularly in larger American cities anxious to bring in development one may find what is termed the growth machine. (Logan and Molotch, 2007) The concept of the growth machine is all about land use and the relationship between developers as private sector entrepre-neurs and local governments. It has the potential to encourage unethical behavior among some public officials. Since land use policy making is the most important policy a local government can make according to land use expert William Waugh and is extraordinarily lucrative to land develop-ers there is a great deal at stake with land use development. The close relationship between developers and policymakers can exacerbate public employee unethical decisions. which gives private land use developers an upper hand in developing their own policies at the expense of public input. (Logan and Molotch, 2007, p. p. 63-67)

The growth machine presents three important ethical questions and con-cerns: first, who is responsible for making public policy? Is it the local government or an unknown number of private concerns? Second, with the enormous pressure from all the components of the growth machine are public decisionmakers likely to make some serious mistakes. Finally, the growth machine brings about the dilemma of economic development versus local government environmental responsibility. Local governments want and need economic development, but as whose expense?

Non-government elites play a major role in electing local politicians, 'watch-dogging' their activities and scrutinizing administrative detail. In turn some officials give a special hand to those entrepreneurs with whom that politician has a special relationship" (Logan and Molotch, 2007, p. p. 63–67). Such policymakers includes government officials who have control over land use policy. This puts commercial property owners into the role of outside individuals who must influence government decisions. Making campaign contributions to the "right" local officials seems to be the most often used method to gain this sort of influence. (Molotch and Logan, 2007, p.p. 63-67)

This ethical question brought up by Logan and Molotch is particularly acute because it is so widespread. To turn such an important policy over to private individuals or organizations who benefit from land use policies at the expense of the control of legitimate representatives of the local populations or the people themselves is not consistent with what a democratic society deems ethical. It is not that the growth machine is in and of itself unethical. It is the pressure put on local politicians who are happy to stay away from issues that might offend growth machine interests." (Logan and Molotch, 2007, p. 64)

There is no reason why local government decision-makers cannot act in a fair impartial manner in determining the best economic development policy while working with the growth machine. In spite of the pressures from the growth machine, in the end most employees who deal directly with economic development are honest and make well throughout decisions.

PRESSURE AND ETHICAL BEHAVIOR IN SINGLE PURPOSE GOVERNMENTS

So far, this chapter has concentrated on general purpose local government interest group pressure. But this is only part of the story of the nearly 90,000 local governments in this country. (Phillips, 2010, p. 441) About 38,500 of these have been created for one single purpose. (Federalism US, 2017) These forms of governments operate as districts, public corporations or authorities. (Note 3) Because they constitute more than half of all the local governments it is important that they also are being considered in this chapter. (Neumark, 2023, p.p. 8-11) Are the pressures affecting the decision making and operation of single purpose governments any different from those found in general-purpose local governments? Although not perfect and fraught with its own set of problems, districts, public corporations, or authorities can distance their employees from some of the everyday pressures, including hyperpluralism. Because their mission is to provide only one service, there are many fewer issue networks pulling the employees every which way. This may very well relieve some of the stress these policy makers may face. They can also be more responsive to their constituents (Sonoma County, California, 2003.)

On the other hand, since single purpose governments are more hidden from the public. Many of us have no idea who the policy makers or legislators are in the myriad of authorities and districts which are in every corner of this country. Being in the shadows could lead to less stress but the possibility of single purpose policy makers who may take advantage of being out of the public spotlight. They can be less accountable. (Ortez, n.d.)

Does less stress, but being more in the shadows actually have an effect on employees for these forms of government? Are their officials necessarily more or less ethical? In a recent study in California, a commission empowered by the state's senate to study the ethical behavior of single purpose governments found that the vast number of individuals working for these governments are conscientious and hard working. (Ortiz, n.d.)

Single purpose governments are not completely out of the shadows. No matter what degree of independence a single purpose government may have, they are still under the oversight of the federal as well as their state governments. The 1939 Hatch Act sets forth a set of public employees ethical rules and regulations for all levels and types of government. (U.S.O.S.C., 1924) The general public may not be aware of what behaviors go on in single purpose governments; and their issue networks may not be as widespread; however, those organizations and individuals with a reason to contact a single purpose government certainly know to whom to turn. (Or find out in a hurry) And except for districts, the ethical conduct of their employees under pressure from the outside is always under the scrutiny of another general-purpose government. (Note 7) There is no evidence that employees of single purpose governments maintain any less ethical behavioral standards than their other government counterparts in spite of what pressures they may receive.

CONCLUSION

Public organizations as well as those in the private sector have every right to look out for their own interests. That's not in question. The ethical problem lies when government employees are under so much pressure from so many outside sources they become so overwhelmed that they take the easy way out and they make rash decisions, or they turn policy control over to one or more of the special interest groups.

Pressures on American government employees come from all corners of society. Although stress has occurred throughout our history, there has been a change in more recent times. With revolutionary level advancements in technology and communication, what may have started out as traditional pluralism has ballooned into hyperpluralism. The number of interest groups pulling government employees every which way has exploded.

The ethical question of hyperpluralism comes to the surface when such a large number of factions become so influential that a government becomes unable to function properly. It is an exaggerated, or even a perverted form of traditional American pluralism. (Longly, 2021). It becomes a case where government and private organizations enter into collusion to capture the policy making process to the clear detriment of our democracy. (Dahl, 1961). Hyperpluralism affects all levels of governments. In spite of the pressures the vast majority of government employees are honest hardworking individuals. The dangers are always lurking, however.

Hyperpluralism also boils down to the public. Our obligation is to continue to make sure our public officials make honest and well-thought-out decisions. The pressures on governments will unlikely ease anytime soon. Government employees and the public will have to function together within this environment.

NOTES

Note 1: This chapter uses the term groups generically. In reality, the term groups should be separated from the term organizations. Both are collections of individuals; however, what one properly refers to as a group may have no membership boundaries, no specific governance, and are often less permanent. Organizations constitute a specialized form of groups having a specific membership criterion as well as a definite governance. Traditional pluralist theory has not normally included groups in their studies of the political process.

Note 2: Issue networks are those individuals, groups and organizations involved in influencing the establishment of a specific policy. They are very fluid and often break apart once the policy has been decided. The concept of issue networks runs counter to the idea of iron triangles, which posits that policy is made by a combination of executive bureaus, congressional committees, and outside interest groups. (Adams, 1981) They are referred to as iron triangles because the average citizen is left out and cannot penetrate the specific policy making process. Issue networks are more democratic and are consistent with a traditional pluralist model.

Note 3: Districts and authorities in particular are single purpose governments. (Some public corporations are also included as governments.) They are similar; however, there are some significant differences. Both are established to perform a specific service such as water/sewer or transportation services. Even though they are their own governments, while districts are independent, authorities are often a branch of another government. Both fit the definition of any governmental political unit, including police powers and eminent domain. They are normally found on the state or local levels. (Neumark, 2023, p.p. 8-11) Although established to deliver one service, some of the larger authorities provide a number of services. For example, the New York and New Jersey Ports Authority controls shipping in New York Harbor, they also manage three airports in New York, New Jersey, and are involved in real estate which have no specific connection to ports. In one particular major American city, in its central business district, besides the one general purpose local government, there are twenty-four other single purpose governments. (Neumark, 2023, p.p. 8-11)

CONCEPTS FOR THOUGHT OR RESEARCH

Ad-hoc groups
Alienation of control
Authorities
Best possible policy
Coalitions
Districts
General purpose governments
Growth Machine
Groups
Hatch Act
Hyperpluralism
Incrementalism
Influence
Interest groups

Iron Triangle
Issue Networks
MARTA
Neo pluralism
Organizations
Political elites
Political pluralism
Polyarchy
Public corporations
Single purpose governments
Special interest groups
Traditional pluralism
Who Governs?

REFERENCES

Adams, Gordon. (1981). *The Politics of Defense Contracting.* Oxfordshire, England, U.K. Routledge.

Birkland, T. A. (2011). *An Introduction to the Policy Process Theories, Concepts, and Models of Public Policy Making.* New York: Routledge.

Dahl, R. A. (1961) *Who Governs?* New Haven, CT: Yale University Press.

———. (1983). *Dilemmas of Pluralist Democracy: Autonomy vs. Control.* New Haven, CT: Yale University Press.

Dye, T. R. and B. H. Sparrow. (2009). *Politics in America* (8th ed.) New York: Longman.

Federalism US. (2020) "1.1 Number of Government Jurisdictions" https//: federalism.us/significantfeatures2020. Accessed: May 6, 2024.

Heclo, H. (1995) "Issue Networks and the Executive Establishment." D. McCool (ed). *Public Policy Theories, Models, and Concepts an Anthology.* Upper Saddle River, NJ: Printice Hall. P.p. 262-287.

Incerti, T. (2024). "Countering Capture in Local Politics: Evidence from Eight Field Experiments." *The Journal of Politics,* 86 (4). P.p. 1603 – 1607.

Lindblom, C. E. (1950). "The Science of Muddling Through." *Public Administration Review,* 19. p.p. 79-88.

Logan, J. R., and H. L. Molotch. (2007). *Urban Fortunes the Political Economy of Place.* 20th Anniversary ed. Berkeley, CA: University of California Press.

Longly, R. (2021). "What Is Hyperpluralism? Definition and Examples." https://www.Thoughtco.com/hyperpluralism-definition-and-examples-5200855. Accessed: April 11, 2024.

Mc Farland, A. S. 2004. *Neopluralism the Evolution of Political Process Theory.* Lawrence, Kansas: The University of Kansas Press.

Norman, R. (nd). "The Idea of Pluralism in the United States." Ourpluralhistory.stcc.edu/Resources/Curriculum/TheIdeofPluralism.pdf. Accessed: April 16, 2024.

Ortez, D. (n.d.) "Integrity & Accountability: Exploring Special Districts' Governance." https://sonomalafco.org>reports-and-publications. Accessed: April 29, 2024.

Phillips, E. B. (2010). *City Lights Urban-Suburban life in the Global Society.* New York: Oxford University Press.

Sonoma County, California Local Agency Formation Commission. (2003) "Integrity & Accountability : Exploring Special Districts Governance." https://sonomalafco.org> Reports-and-publications. Accessed: April 25, 2024.

Truman, D. (1951). *The Governmental Process*. New York: Knopf.

U.S.0.C.S. (United State Office of Special Council. (1924) "Hatch Act Overview." osc.gov/Service/Pages/HatchAct.aspx. Accessed: September 28, 2024.

ETHICAL DELIVERY OF SOCIAL SERVICES IN THE UNITED STATES

7

INTRODUCTION

The delivery of important social services also brings about possible ethics issues faced by local public officials. Up until now, we have looked at more general behavioral ethics. In this chapter we will take a closer look at the ethical dilemma posed by a very specific local public policies.

Social services are something that the American public does not always think about, and yet most of us are the recipients in one way or another. We may also not be aware that there is any sort of conflict between our local governments and their social service delivery policies. But there are, and they produce ethical dilemmas. The main conflict is over the questions who and how vital public services should be provided. These questions are inherent in our free-market society (Gold, 2002, p. 209).   Should local governments relinquish their role in supplying these important services? And if so, where does the role of ethics enter the picture?

American social services

Important social services include the mix of programs and direct services intended to help individuals in need. In the United States, they are normally recognized as:

- Food and nutrition
- Health advice and disease prevention
- Hospital services
- Mental health support
- Public financial assistance
- Child support
- Child protection services
- Adult protection services
- Adoption/foster care
- Disabled services
- Education

(Wall, 2014, p. 665)

Because of the tradition of public/private partnerships, social service delivery in the United States may be quite different than those provided by governments in other countries. (Note 1) The main point of departure is over the question of should the government or the private sector provide social services. And if the provision is most appropriate by government, should it come from the local, state or federal. Whether one feels that vital services must be delivered by the governments or private organizations, the one point of agreement is our American public deserves the highest level of fairness and ethical treatment by the provider. The answers to all of the questions are at the very heart of the social service conflict and concern about what is and what is not ethical.

SOCIAL SERVICES OR SOCIAL WORK?

The delivery of social services and social work, which is only one aspect of social services are not the same. Social work is often the way social services are delivered. Although our focus is on the delivery of social services, social workers have their own code of ethics developed by the National Association of Social Workers (NASW). Notice how closely these ethical standards tie into their service delivery ethos.

- Carrying out the highest standards of service to people in need
- Social justice
- Uphold the dignity and worth of their clients

- Uphold the importance of human relationships
- Uphold the highest level of integrity
- Uphold the highest level of competence
- Uphold their responsibility to clients at all times
- Always act as professionals

(NASW, 2021)

Because social service policies and social work are so intertwined, much of the ethical concerns expressed in this chapter will apply to both.

PUBLIC, PRIVATE, OR DOES IT MATTER?

Are there any ethical differences between the private or public provision of social services? There are differences; however, they may not necessarily be unethical.

The case for private delivery of social services: economic and efficiency

The idea of who should deliver social services may boil down to an economic question. A private producer may have the greater economic means and would be consistent with the economic principle of Pareto optimality. (the most cost-efficient delivery of services) Private organizations may not suffer from the cutbacks and restraints imposed on governments on all levels. Local governments in this country are in a period of constant fiscal restraint. (Urhan, 2012) In some states county and local governments cannot constitutionally go into debt. Thus, many of our local governments have been forced into cutbacks. Many counties and local governments simply cannot afford to provide the increased service demands. The diminishment of services brings up two concerns, one directly related to the ethics of equal service delivery: how local governments will determine who may and who may not receive a particular service. The other is, if the government cannot provide and important social service, who will? Should the responsibility be turned over to the state government or to a private organization? Budget constraints are one of the main reason why many local governments are turning to private provision of essential services.

Even if the local government can afford a service, there are those who believe that private provision of services is simply more cost effective. Those governments turning to privatization look at that policy as a way of balancing budgets while maintaining a minimum but tolerable level of service. (Goodman and Loveman, 1991).

Another reason why a number of local governments are turning to the private delivery of social services is efficiency. Some governments and their citizens believe that privatization is more efficient in the ability to provide services. In a recent survey of Americans, two-thirds believe that the private sector employees work harder than public sector employees. (Katz, 2013) In most cases, the harder employees work, the more efficient the output. This, however, may be more perception than reality.

The case for public delivery of social services

Private delivery of social services may not be a panacea. There are some significant advantages of the social services which may be provided by local or county governments. (Note 2) They include:

- Lower costs due to the economies of scale (Note 3)
- More highly regulated, particularly by state governments
- Greater accessibility to all clients
- More equal in the service delivery
- More community focused

(Based on Hassell, 2021)

Social responsibility

An additional view is that governments not a private producer have the only mandate and social responsibility to provide for a service delivery. For a private producer to do so is inherently not ethical (Wrigley and McKevitt, 1998, p.p. 71–73). Their point is based upon the economic notion that social service delivery should be considered a public good. Which means that the consumer cannot be left out. A private for-profit service deliverer will normally define the service as a market good and may choose to leave out the consumer who does not have the where-with-all to pay for that service. A private organization may decide that one's ability to pay should be the basis of the service delivery. Individuals who are in greatest need may simply be denied because they cannot pay.

Local governments are much more hesitant to deny the services to any of its citizens because of any personal economic issues. They also are much more likely to consider social services a public good. Pareto optimality is less important than the equitable delivery of social services. Wrigley and McKevitt call the public provision of social service the ethics of social responsibility: "Historically, for the provision of important social services, government has explicitly or implicitly been held out as the institution which is an alternative to the market in the allocation of resources" (Wrigley and McKevitt, 1998, p. 760).

To the extent that the ethical delivery of public services is based on fair service to all, there is no clear evidence that either view is more correct. Both sectors have their advantages as well as disadvantages. The majority of social service organizations strive to be as ethical as possible.

Education, a special case of social responsibility

Of all the various types of social services, education as a social service perhaps touches the most Americans. We all go through the educational process to a varying extent, and many of us have children who are now in school. Because it affects so many Americans and there are so many unanswered questions and differing points of views regarding education, it may also be the most controversial of the social services. What is best for our children? There are so many questions and disagreements. Of interest to this chapter, is a matter of ethics. Are there any unethical practices surrounding educational services? So many questions, so few answers.

- Should I send my child to a public or private school?
- Should I send my child to a religious school?
- Should the government pay for my child's private or religious education?
- Does my local school provide a quality challenging education? If not, which schools in my community have a reputation for the highest quality? And can I even send my child there?

- Should I move to a different local community (vote with my feet)?
- Will my child be bullied in my local school?
- As a minority, will there be equality for my child in his or her education?
- Will there be students who disrupt my child's classes? And if so, what will the school do about it?
- My child has special needs, will he or she be given a full opportunity to learn?
- My child has a different way of learning, what provisions will be made for him or her?

These are all very real, and serious, and difficult questions that many American families face. In the end parents expect fair, transparent, and ethical behavior from those delivering their educational services.

Although education questions are normally private family concerns, they are not entirely without government involvement. Normally, education policy is the responsibility of the state but carried out by a local government. No matter which level of government develops the policies, the public has the right to demand ethical responsibility . The cornerstone of public ethical behavior is for government employees to actively strive to do what is right for **everyone.** (Rabinowitz, nd.) Education services are no different.

In the following true case study, based on a state's current education policy, the questions considered are is that policy completely ethical. Is it doing whatever it can to make sure that **all of their students** receive the highest and best education possible? Is the state practicing responsible social public policy? The policy presents an educational dilemma spreading throughout the country: is allowing students in underperforming schools free access to other educational programs?

CASE STUDY 7.1: A STATE'S EDUCATION VOUCHER POLICY

In one of the larger states, under the leadership of the governor the legislature has established an expanded school voucher (scholarship) policy enacted for the 2023-2024 school year. Every student, for any reason, can now obtain a voucher to allow that student to attend any other public or private school of his or her choice without having to state a reason. The policy makes all resident students eligible to receive taxpayer backed vouchers up to $8,000 per year to attend any school in which they are accepted. (NBC Miami 2023).

Supporters of the policy believe that vouchers provide competition among schools, which will raise the quality of education. The governor stated that the policy will put parents and students first and give them freedom. (NBC Miami, 2023) (Note 4)

On the surface this policy seems fair. After all, it applies to any and every student. But is it fair? A close examination of the policy calls the ethics of the policy into question. If all students had equal ability to access the vouchers, there would be no question about the ethical responsibility. But this is not the case. There are those students whose parents cannot supply transportation to a different school for any myriad of reasons or do not have the time to do so. As long as these students attend their local school, they have bus transportation or they can walk, but the state's policy does not offer transportation if they choose to use a voucher. (Note 5) Only those students whose parents have the financial means, and time can take advantage of the voucher policy. The remainder of the students are left to their own resources.

The outcome of this policy has made it possible for wealthier children to be able to attend a school of their choice. It has served to become an entitlement for wealthy children. The majority of new vouchers were awarded to students whose families make as much as $250,000 a year. Nearly half of the new enrollees in the expanded voucher program (53,828 students) are above the previous income level for obtaining the voucher. (Ressenger, 2023)

The other question concerns using public tax monies for private or religious education. Is it ethical for the state to use taxpayer money for the benefit of private or religious organizations?   For example, what if the only private school in a community is a Christian church sponsored school, but the student is Jewish, Hindu, or Moslem? If one agrees with Rabinowitz that the state's school policy is not right for everyone, under practical circumstances, not all students will not, or cannot be treated equally, in spite of their parents having to pay for the benefits of the policy through taxation, then the ethics of the policy can be called into question. (Chasnow, 2023) Others agree: school voucher policies can be dangerous to American education. They produce unequal access to high-quality schools as well as segregation. (Cowen, 2022) (Note 6)

The question is not whether or not private schools provide a better education than public schools. There are some outstanding private schools as well as some that are subpar. The same can be said for public schools. The two real questions boil down to ethics. Is it ethical to provide public monies to students in situations where there cannot be the equal distribution of the benefits? And is it ethical to use public funds for the benefit of private (or religious) institutions even though any student may attend?

- Is there something you would do as a board of education member for those students who are kept in failing schools once all the families who were able to choose to had left?
- If your child were in a failing school, how would you feel about vouchers?
- What would you do to insure that your child receives the very best education possible?
- Is every citizen of the state being equally in both the execution as well as the outcome?

UNDER WHAT CIRCUMSTANCES ARE THE PRIVATE DELIVERY OF A SOCIAL SERVICES MORE ETHICAL?

Earlier in the chapter we noted that there is no research evidence to suggest that either the public or the private delivery of social services is more ethical than the other. As long as the government responsible for the service is astute and keeps a close eye on the service delivery, there is no reason why it cannot be provided by a private organization, or perhaps even another government.

In reality, it depends on who has the greatest resources to extend a specific social service to the public. Smaller cities and counties may not be able to deliver every needed service adequately. Specialized private organizations may be able to do a much better job and as ethically as one should expect from a government. Conversely, If one agrees with the view that social services should be considered a public good, it should only be delivered directly by the government. (Wrigley and Mc Kevitt, 1998, p. 760)

As this disagreement continues there are, however, a few ethical questions which must be addressed: is everyone entitled to the service treated equally? Can the private organization provide the service as well or better than the local government? Is any fee for that service completely fair? And who will regulate the service. If the answer is yes to these questions then there is no ethical reason why a private organization cannot provide the social service.

CONCLUSION

The provision of social services is one of the most important aspects of local and county governments. There is no evidence that overall, the public departments as well as private agencies delivering the services do not do an ethical job.

This country, if not the whole free world, however, are facing the reality that the demand for many of the social service programs is out stripping the government's resources. (Population Matters, 2024) How can our local governments continue to provide a high level of service in a period of economic cutbacks? A common way of solving this dilemma is through privatization. Although social services are legally mandated, privatization means that the government is no longer in full control, which then brings up a number of ethical questions. First and perhaps most important, can a private organization refuse to provide a service if an individual cannot pay? How much oversight does the government have when they choose a private provider to make sure that every citizen is treated equally? And do private service providers necessarily do a more efficient job in reaching the clients than can a government?

The thread going through all of these questions is all about equal treatment. If we agree that the ethics of social services lie in treating every citizen equally, one can understand why it is so important for a government to make sure that whoever is the provider, a social service must follow the highest and fair ethical manner.

Educational services in the United States are a special case since it touches so many Americans. The ethical problem here is the more recent momentum towards private providers of education paid for by public money. Whether a student receives a public or private education is not the question. Neither is whether or not private institutions provide better educational services than public schools. It is a parent's private decision regarding where their child will go to school. The ethical issue arises when a government uses tax money to pay for a child's private education. The most common way is through vouchers (scholarships) for the student to choose any public or private institution other than their locally zoned school. How can governments insure that every child is treated equally under voucher policy? The issue arises with the ability of only some families who are able to take advantage of school vouchers.

Every ethical question posed in this chapter concerned policies made by individuals. If you are reading this book, there is a good chance that you may be a public policy decisionmaker perhaps in the field of social service delivery. If you agree that past policy decisions have been completely ethical then it will be your job to continue these policies. However, if you feel that the ethics of the current policies are questionable, then it becomes your job as a policymaker to do your part in making sure that unethical policies are eliminated.

The current social service dilemma in an era of local governmental budget constraints and spending priorities is does the government expend limited resources on fewer programs with service to a smaller population, or does a government leave it up to a private organization to supply the service with the ability to limit the population receiving the service? It is a difficult question, but one which must be answered with the issue of ethics in mind.

NOTES

Note 1: To prevent ambiguity, this chapter will classify not for profit social service providers as private organizations since they are not an actual branch of government.

Note 2: Although county governments are branches of state governments, in many states they are the only local municipal government. Also in some states the city government is allowed to provide social services, while in others, it is up to the county. In other states, counties share the provision of social services, with their cities, towns and townships.

Note 3: Economies of scale: the more of a certain item is purchased, the lower the unit price of that item.

Note 4: When the governor stated that the policy puts students and parents first, he never mentioned "first" over what or whom. Neither did he mention what he meant by his use of the term "freedom."

Note 5: In a real sense, this was the question in Brown v. Topeka Board of Education. Since the plaintiff was not provided with equal transportation to school and was forced to walk past the closest school, the Supreme Court decided that education policy in Topeka, Kansas was inherently unequal. In the words of Rabinowitz, the board of education did not provide the plaintiff with ethical responsibility.

Note 6: This state is only one with this policy. Almost fifty states now have some variant of a school voucher program. (Chasnow, 2023)

CONCEPTS FOR THOUGHT OR RESEARCH

Budget constraints	Political conflicts in education
Dwindling governmental resources	Privatization
Economies of scale	Private sector
Ethics of social responsibility	Public good
Free market society	School vouchers (school choice)
Market good	Social services
Pareto optimality	Social work

REFERENCES

Chasanov, D. (2023). "Bias Unethical: Educators Upset About O.S.E.D. Sharing School Choice Information Online." https://ktul.com/newsletter-daily-/biased-Unethical-educators-upset-about-osde-sharing-school-choice-information-Online. Accessed: May 23, 2024.

Gold, H. (2002.) *Urban Life and Society.* Upper Saddle River, N. J. Prentice Hall.

Cowen, J. (2022). "Opinion: After Two Decades of Studying Voucher Programs I'm Now Firmly Opposed to Them." https://hechingerreport.org/opinion-after-two-decades-of-studying-voucher-programs-im-now-firmly-opposed-to-them/. Accessed: May 22, 2024.

Goodman, J. B. and G. W. Loveman. (2091). "Does Privatization Serve the Public Interest"? https://hbr.org/1991/11/does-privatization-serve-the-public-interest. Accessed: May 17, 2024.

Hassell, T. (2024). "The Benefits of Public Behavioral Health Care." https://www.wtpsp.org/whats-the-difference-between-public-and-privste-behvioral-health-care/ Accessed: May 13, 2024.

Katz, E. (2013) "Poll-Americans Think Private Sector Works Harder Than Public Sector." www.govexec.com/pay-benefits/2023/02/poll-americans-think-private-sector-works-harder-public-sector/61218/. Accessed: May 18, 2024.

NASW. (2021) https://www.socialworkers.org/About/Ethics/Code-of-Ethics-English. Accessed: May 13, 2024

NBC Miami. (2023). https://www.nbcmiami.com/news/local/floridas-expanded-School-voucher-system-explained-whats-changed-and-whos-eligible/3/04/356/. Accessed: May 19, 2024.

Population Matters. (2024). "Global Resources are Dwindling as Demand Rises." populationmatters.org/news/2024/03/global-resources-dwindling-as-demand-rises/ Accessed: October 7. 2024.

Rabinowitz, P. (nd) https://ctb.ku.edu/en/table-of-contents/analyze/choose-and-Adapt-community-interventions-ethical-issues/main. Accessed: May 19, 2024.

Ressenger, J. (2024). "2023: The Year School Vouchers Became an Entitlement for Wealthy Children." https://nepc.colorado.edu>blogyear-school. Accessed: May 21, 2024.

Urhan, S. K. (2012). Falling Revenues and Growing Demand for Services Challenge Cities, Counties, and School Districts. Pewtrusts.org/en/research-and-analysis/reports/000/01/01/the-local-squeeze. Accessed: February 3, 2025.

Wall, N. A. (2014). https://www.sog.unc/sites/default/files/course/materials/Cmg%2039_SocialServices_1.pdf. Accessed:10, 2024.

Wrigley, L. and D. McKevitt. (1998.) "Professional Ethics Government Agenda and Differential Information." In *Public Sector Management Theory, Critique & Practice*, David McKevitt and Alan Lawton (eds). London, England, UK: Sage Publications. 71- 84.

ETHICAL BEHAVIOR AND TECHNOLOGY

INTRODUCTION

We are in the middle of the "technological revolution." For most of us the growth of technology has been very positive. There are, of course, those who have not benefited as much as others. Technological innovations seem to change every day. Think back as little as ten years ago and compare your use of technology to the second decade of the twenty-first century.

Other than individuals hacking into computer systems or other illegal activities such as "phishing," we do not often think how public ethics is connected to the use of technology. However, there is an important connection between these two often overlooked aspect of government employee behavior.

Examples of the most modern forms of technology

Although we may be stating the obvious, here are some examples of modern technology to name a few, many of which have a direct connection to governmental services:

- Desk top computers
- Tablets

- Artificial Intelligence (AI)
- Personal computers
- Desk and wall telephones
- Smart phones
- Personal video connections (Zoom, Teams . . .etc.)
- Fire sticks
- Personal movie subscriptions
- Medical chairs which can weigh the patient and take his or her blood pressure.
- Direction finders (WAZE)
- Hundreds of social media sites
- Robotic surgery
- LED lights
- Compact fluorescent lights

On the other hand, there are technologies which became popular in recent years and now are on their way out in just the past few years:

- Compact disks and payers
- Computers with towers
- Personal film cameras
- Personal digital cameras (Note 1)
- Some social media sites such as "MY Space."
- Flip-phones

Although not all of the technologies in the above lists have a direct relevance to government services they are meant to paint a picture of the world in which our governments exist. For governments to not keep up with technology, according to Professor Greg Streib, is in and of itself unethical. The use of technology by public officials, as with all forms of behavior, must comport with public ethics.

PRIVATE VERSUS PUBLIC USE OF TECHNOLOGY

Private use of technology

Although this book is not concerned with the private use of technology, this section is included to highlight the difference between private and public technical uses in the workplace. There is a clear difference. Unless an individual's use of private technology is blatantly illegal, such as downloading illegal websites, or using one's technology to hack into others', no one pays much attention to what individuals do in their own offices. How many of us would really be upset to learn that a private organization employee uses his or her lunchtime to play games on the company computer, or the company telephone to make private hotel reservations or other calls having nothing to do with the business? The private organization managers (if they themselves don't do the same thing) may not be too happy, but the rest of us would more than likely just shrug it off: "It's not our business." One may be frustrated having to endure artificial intelligence when trying to contact a bank or talk to a real human being from private companies' customer service department, but at the same time, we understand that it is their right to operate their business in whichever way they choose. We may not be so understanding when the same thing happens when trying to contact out local governments. The real difference in our attitude towards private or public use of technology lies in our expectations of the public sector.

Public use of technology

Many more of us may not appreciate it if it came to light that a public official was using official technological equipment for personal reasons during (or perhaps even after) work time. After all, this is the public's equipment. Our expectations are that government employees will use their government owned equipment the most judiciously.

Although one may believe that some of the unethical technological practices discussed below may be more serious than others, nevertheless most fall short of what the public holds to be the high standards of our public officials. Because many of these minor but still unethical behaviors are so widely practiced, it is possible that many public servants are even unaware that some of them may be inconsistent with local ethical codes they are worth mentioning. The problem with disregarding minor ethical lapses is at what point does a minor ethical infraction become major? Where does one draw the line?

MISUSES OF PUBLIC TECHNOLOGY

Unauthorized websites

Of all the possible misuses of government owned technology, the most common is for public employees to use their publicly issued equipment for their own private purposes. Being so widespread does not make it more ethical. This normally includes telephones or computers: for example, visiting a website that is not work related on or off work hours at the job or at home.

Admittedly how widespread this practice may be in the public sector is difficult to trace. A technologically savvy individual can be quite secretive and most public managers probably do not check up on their employees to that extent. If an employee is caught on an unacceptable website or making a private call it is most likely by accident.

Refusal or unable to use technology

In a recent discussion with the author, Professor Gregory Streib brought up a subtler, less obvious connection between technology and ethics: a public employee's refusal to use or being unable to use technology to communicate with his or her constituents. Streib posits that for a public official not to know and be able to use the state-of-the-art technology, or simply refuses to use technology for whatever reason, is by his definition unethical. He uses the example of the public employee who regularly refuses to answer or return telephone calls simply because that person does not want to be bothered either by someone that that official may regard as a critic, or a constituent constantly wanting a favor. There are some government employees who think they are too important to be bothered. Or is that public servant trying to hide something? Streib's contention is that a public servant cannot be ethical if he or she is unable or unwilling to give members of the public needed information or a service, including a one-on-one conversation. It doesn't matter whether or not a public employee believes that some requested information may be unimportant, it is that person's job to communicate with his or her constituents. Gross (2021) refers to this obligation as "courtesy expectations." Perhaps, few, if any, public officials consider this refusal as an important component of their obligation to the public. However, think how a constituent may feel if what he or she considers an important call is never returned.

Not using technology equally to all segments of the public

With equal service to all of the constituents regardless of economic, social, or political standing as an important hallmark of governmental ethics, the concern is how do they serve an entire population as they increasingly rely on technology. Not everyone has equal access to technology. (Felbinger, 2013, p. 158). The reality is those individuals who have better access to modern technology are in a much better position to demand and receive public services. Just think about how affective, quick or efficient texting or emailing can be, but not everyone has the ability to join in on the "electronic revolution." The inability of one segment to demand and receive the same level of services as other individuals who have technology at their fingertips can result in the uneven distribution of governmental programs. Many of us can easily pick up our phones or computers (no matter where we happen to be at a given time) to contact a local official over a problem, but governmental agencies do not always make it easy for those without modern technology to communicate with them. How many times have you tried to reach your government over some issue only to be told that you would be better served to email in or text your request? Many of us have been put on hold for a half hour or more waiting to speak to some government agency. We don't always have that sort of time. If public agencies are biased in favor of those who have better access to the electronic revolution then governments are not meeting their ethical obligation to the entire population.

The following is a true case study based on the experience of an individual who did not have the requisite technology in order to park in Downtown Columbus, Ohio:

CASE STUDY 8.1: PARK COLUMBUS: ACCESSIBLE AND EQUITABLE?

Recently, the City of Columbus, Ohio initiated a new parking system using the most up-to-date technology. Instead of the "old fashion" parking meters, the new system is based on smartphone apps. Those with smartphones download the app and follow the instructions to pay for the particular parking space in the city's downtown. The system is administered by Park Columbus.

According to the Park Columbus Mission Statement "The Division of Parking Services is committed to providing **accessible, equitable, and predictable** mobility and parking options for all residents, **guests**, and **visitors**." (Columbus, 2024) What this out of town person found is that the new parking system is neither equitable, widely accessible, nor guest friendly.

For two years in a role, while visiting downtown, the individual could not park in the area even though spaces were available. The problem is that she does not have a smartphone. She does not have the parking app. On the parking instructions posted on the streets, it does say that if one does not have the app, one can call a specific telephone number. However, on both occasions, no one answered the posted telephone number. In the end she left and simply did not visit that area.

Since the individual does not visit Columbus regularly she felt that there was no personal loss. (The only loss was to the city in parking revenue.) But what about those who live in the area and cannot visit downtown because they are unable or unwilling to obtain a smartphone or use their app? The city's government says in their own words **accessible** and **equitable**. To some, however, parking in the area is neither. The city government has failed in its obligation to provide an equal service to everyone: **residents and visitors alike.**

Cincinnati, Ohio and Chattanooga, Tennessee have similar parking systems; however, in both cases they include alternate parking sys-

- Have you ever been in a technological Catch 22?
- How would you design a parking system which took advantage of the latest technology and yet was completely equal and fair to everyone?
- Do you think governments charging for parking is inherently unfair?

Whether or not one may ever visit the city of Columbus is not the point. Someone in the city's government proposed this policy, which does not fulfill its obligations to serve all equally.

The development of public policy presents an ethical dilemma. Governments are expected to operate as efficiently as possible, which means adopting the latest technological innovations. At the same time there are those citizens who for whatever reason do not themselves keep up with technology. Yet it is the government's obligation to serve as much of their constituency as possible. As a future or present government policy maker, how would you include those individuals who simply do not have the same ability to access government?

LOOKING TOWARDS THE FUTURE: ARTIFICIAL INTELLINGENCE (AI) TECHNOLOGY AND PUBLIC ETHICS

No one can predict the future, although it is certainly obvious that the continued advancement in technology, particularly in artificial intelligence (AI) technology will take center stage. This section looks at some of the possible ethical concerns connected with this quickly expanding technical advancements as it affects the ethical relationship between citizens and their local governments. Technology can be a double-edged sword. With any new rapid advancements, it is important to foster its advantages but also be aware of what expected or unexpected ethical concerns may crop up.

Artificial intelligence (AI) and ethics

Arguably, the most controversial technological advancement is the growth of artificial intelligence. The reality is that AI is seeping into all aspects of life, from our personal homes to our local governments. As society discovers increasing uses of this technology, (besides answering telephones) it has the potential to revolutionize government services for the better, but also possibly for the worse. Government employees and the public are going to have to understand and deal with artificial intelligence.

It may be way too soon to gauge the effects of AI on society, but it is helpful to include what some of the experts are saying about this revolutionary technology in its early stages especially as it concerns ethics. As you read through this section keep in mind that what is being written today may entirely change tomorrow.

The advent of artificial intelligence has the ability of changing every aspect of human life.   From the outset, it is important to state that there is nothing in and of itself unethical about AI. And it's here to stay. The ethical questions involved are how this technology is used.

One of the ethical worries concerning AI is that governments are behind in their understanding of the possible negative effects of artificial intelligence (Pazzanese, 2020). The challenges of AI are much like the challenges presented by any new technology, but most governments have yet to address its ethical implications. (Bostrom and Yudkowsky, 2011)

Governments themselves may misuse the technology. AI is not limited to hackers and other criminals trying to use it for their own advantages. AI can be intentionally misused to infringe on our rights as Americans through mass surveillance and censorship. (US Department of State, 2024) This misuse is not confined to rogue foreign governments. It has the potential to be found in all levels of government right here in this country. Unfortunately, the track record of public AI use provides a range of evidence of government misuse. (Burton, 2023)

AI has opened new avenues for local governments to enhance resident services and streamline their operations. For example, it allows local governments to optimize operations by automating repetitive tasks, minimizing human errors, and promoting efficiency. However, at the same time, it raises questions about the need for additional oversite, security, and privacy (Civic Plus, 2023). These safeguards have so far not taken place on any widespread level. Local governments may not have the resources to govern AI satisfactorily. It may take the partnership among the local, state, and federal governments to be able to do so. AI may have many possibilities and benefits. However, since it is such a new technology, governments still do not have a handle on how to completely master artificial intelligence or its ethical implications. In time that should come.

Local governments may wish to consider the following possible policy actions in regard to advancements in technology:

- Develop a set of ethical standards in the use of technology which can be adopted by all local governments
- Develop standard technological oversight protocols, including the establishment of citizen and employee oversight boards
- Establish mandatory technological education for all employees on a continuing basis, especially in the use of artificial intelligence.
- Keep up with the latest technology
- Partner with the other local governments as well as other levels of governments such as the state or the federal government in order to provided added resource
- Establish periodic town hall meetings with the general public on the subject of technology
- Research, test, and collaborate with experts and stakeholders to completely understand the ethical implications of new technology

(Piechowski 2018; Neumark 2024)

The four main points of this sample list include standardization, education, collaboration, and citizen participation.

Technology and free elections

One of the most serious public concerns about AI regards our free and fair elections. "Widely accessible artificial tools could fuel the rampant spread of disinformation and create other hazards to democracy." (Panditharatine and Giansiracusa, 2023) It can also be used to jam the American electoral process. (WSB-TV, 2024) A recent poll found that well over half of Americans worry that AI will be used to spread false and misleading information in the 2024 election campaigns. (Trish, 2024)

Another concern is voting security. Secure internet (online) voting is still impossible. (AAAS, 2020)

In spite of these concerns, some states and local governments appear to be ignoring the "red flags." (Hallene and Allen, 2024) The potential interference with the American free election process is very real. Whether its originates domestically or abroad, technically savvy individuals have tried to use their ability to affect the outcome of a free election to their own advantage. In one recent week, the Georgia Secretary of State's office reported that they were able to fend off 240,000 cyber-attacks on their voter website. (WSB-TV, 2024) The office believes the attacks originated from foreign countries. Russian interference has been confirmed in other elections, which underscores the threat of foreign meddling in American politics. (Trish, 2024) On the positive side, election officials have been able to use technology to fend off these attempted attacks.

The unethical use of unethical technology is not limited to outsiders. We think of individuals outside of government as the possible culprits. But what about an insider who is able to hack into or change an election to protect his or her job or political outlook? Insider hacking has also become an ethical issue which must be closely watched.

The purpose of this section is to not sound the alarm. What we are suggesting is that governments need to become increasingly proactive in dealing with artificial intelligence. The fact that states have become increasingly able to fend off attacks is a positive sign for their own use of technology. Local governments must work hand-in-hand with the state.

THE POSITIVE SIDE OF TECHNOLOGY

The use of public technology with a reasonable amount of caution has been very ethical and positive. Our governments are continuously learning how to combat the unethical use of technology. There have and will be many advantages to technology and its service to citizens. With the proper safeguards, one positive advantage to technology is in the American electoral process. It has not only made voting easier for most Americans: it has enabled those individuals who have limited access to transportation or may be too ill to vote. Although bedridden, former president Jimmy Carter was able to vote in the 2024 election through the process of downloading a ballot and mailing in to his county. (PBS, 2024) (Note: 2) In addition, such innovations as direct recording electronic systems (DRE), optical scanning systems, and internet and mobile systems for example have resulted in significant improvements in the voting process. (Hallene and Allen, 2024)

One of the newer advancements in voting technology is "early voting." Every state, except Alabama, Mississippi, and New Hampshire has taken advantage of this technology. Instead of being confined to a specific precinct, the voter can vote in one of several early voting spots. The computers recognize the residence and produce the correct ballot. It has made voting much easier and quicker. It appears that the electorate is taking advantage of early voting. One state has reported that 55 percent of registered voters have used the technology in the 2024 presidential election. Nationwide, 68 million Americans have voted early. (Pereria, 2024) Two days later, the Reuters press agency reported that the number of early voters jumped to 78 million. (Ferrell, Bavier, Kyvrikosaios, Suleiman, Richter, and Ju-min-Park, 2024) Clearly, the technology which allows voters to be identified anywhere in their county with the correct ballot, has made voting much easier. One can speculate how many of these 78 million would have been discouraged enough by the typical long lines on election day to not vote. There has been no evidence so far to indicate that early voting has been less secure than traditional precinct voting.

Another positive aspect of modern technology is that it makes a public employee's ethical behavior even the more imperative. In an instant, citizens and the media have the ability to trace the behavior of their public leaders. It helps to bring the behavior of public officials out of the shadows.

A well-publicized case of public corruption concerning the government of New York City is underway. (Stratman, 2024) Although the public may not know the extent to which the actions were discovered and investigated by the use of technology, it is reasonable to assume that the State of New York used all the technical means at their disposal to investigate the city's possible unethical actions. If this had happened thirty or more years ago, how easy would it have been to investigate this possible crime? (Note 3)

Technology may not be foolproof, but it becomes more difficult for officials to hide unethical behavior. The result of the increased visibility leads to a higher level of responsibility which raises the quality among these officials (Lorch, 2001, p. 370).

Because today's government organizations are at the forefront of testing technologies and setting standards for their usage, there is an obligation to ensure the protection of their citizens, to promote positive outcomes, and realize the benefits of constantly emerging improvements in technology. (Piechowski, 2018)

Public officials now are more in the spotlight than ever before. Although improvements in technology provides for the ability of citizens to be able to keep track of the behavior of our local government officials who are the most directly responsible for service delivery and to keep those employees on the ethical straight and narrow, at the same time, it is still the responsibility of local citizens to make sure that their governments are acting in the best interests of all of their constituents. Although it is easier now than ever, AI is not going to do it for us!

CONCLUSION

The world is in the middle of a technical revolution, or maybe just starting. All you have to do is to look at the different forms of technology now being used on an everyday basis and ask the question were these being used even as little as ten years ago. Technology can be a wonderful thing, but it also raises ethical questions. Just think about the use of artificial intelligence!

There is a difference in citizen's ethical considerations between the private and public sectors. In the private sector one can use technology in any way the person uses as long as it is legal and is not used for any nefarious purposes. In the public sector the use is only ethical if it is only for the public interest, completely fair to all segments of the population, and is consistent with the obligations set forth by the government. Unfortunately, as outlined in this chapter, there have been a number of ways where governmental behavior regarding technology may not meet the expected highest ethical standards.

The advent and use of artificial intelligence has created an entirely new realm of public technology, both positive and disconcerting. On the one hand, it has made the mission of as well as the delivery of public service so much easier. On the other hand, it brings up the question of who the master is. Of course, it is the shared responsibility of government officials as well as the public to stay on top of the emerging technology.

There are great advantages not only for public officials but for the public to be the masters of all technology. It is now much easier to vote than ever before. The public can obtain ballots from the comfort of their own home, vote early, and vote in a more convenient setting. We have the ability to watch much more closely what our government employees are doing. Modern technology has been able to bring many of the governments operations out of the shadows forcing public employees' behavior to reach a higher ethical level.

Advances in technology are here to stay. We, the public, must use its advantages to continue the job of making sure our governments are acting ethically to of all citizens, including those of you who are reading this chapter.

NOTES

NOTE 1: The use of digital cameras is still in wide use among professional photographers.

NOTE 2: Although the late president Jimmy Carter and others who are similarly situated were able to obtain their ballot online, in his state and in possibly others, the legislatures have made downloading ballots much more difficult. The argument made by the legislatures is that doing so has protected legitimate voters from election fraud.

The counter argument is that there has been no proof of widespread voter fraud through mail in ballots. Those who support the counter argument believe that making the process more difficult has been done for political reasons to keep the opposing political party from voting. Whether one believes that the law really serves to protect voters of all political views, or is meant to dominate one party over another, it makes online voting more difficult. (ACLU, 2023)

Note 3: As this chapter is being written, the United States Justice Department has dropped the charges against the mayor.

CONCEPTS FOR THOUGHT OR RESEARCH

Artificial intelligence (AI)

Direct scanning electronic systems (DRE)

Early voting

Election fraud.

Election interference

Electronic revolution

Ethical use of technology

Equality of public services

Oath of office

Obligation to the public

Online voting

Optical scanning systems

Pay for parking

Parking in Columbus, Ohio

Private use of public technology

Private versus public use of technology

Technological revolution

Technology

Technology and ethics

REFERENCES

AAAS (American Association for the Advancement of Science). (2020). "Internet or Online Voting Remains Insecure." Aaas.org/epicenter/internet-online-voting. Accessed: October 20, 2024.

ACLU. (2023). "Federal Courts Side with Civil Rights Groups and Lifts Georgia's Ban on Online Relief and Birthdate Requirements on Absentee Ballot Envelopes for 2024 Elections." aclu.org/press-releases/federal-court-sides-with-civil-rigfhts-groups-and-lifis-georgias-ban-on-online-relief-and-birthdate-requirements-on-absentee-ballot-envelopes-for-2024-elections. Accessed: October 23, 2024.

Bostrom, N. and E. Yudkowsky. (2011). "The Ethics of Artificial Intelligence." chrome-extension://efaidnbmnnnibpcajpcglclefindmkaj/https://nickbostrom.com/ethics/artificial-intelligence.pdf. Accessed: October 15, 2024.

Burton, J. (2023). "The Real Threat May be the Way that Governments Choose to Use it." theconversation.com/ai-the-real-threat-may-be-the-way-that-governments-choose-to-use-it-216660. Accessed: October 24, 2024.

Civic Plus. (2023). "Artificial Intelligence (AL) and Machine Learning (ML) Security Best Practices for Local Government Systems." https://www.civicplus.com/blog/ce/generative-ai-safety-and-best-prctices-for-local-government-communicators/ Accessed: October 16, 2024.

Columbus, Ohio. (2024). https://www.columbus.gov>services>parking>services. Accessed June 9, 2024.

Felbinger, C. L. (2012). "The City Maintains Itself." In R. Steinbacher and V. O. Benson (Eds.) *Introduction ot Urban Studies* (4th ed.). Dubuque, Iowa: Kendall Hu nt Publishing Company. 145-160.

Gross, S. (2021). "Ethics Codes for Local Governments, Part 1: Considerations, Scope, and Applicability." mrsc.org/stay-informed/mrsc-insight/February-2021/ethics-codes-for-local-governments-part-1. Accessed: October 11, 2024.

Hallene, A. and J. M. Allen. (2024) "The Evolution of Voting Technology." americanbar.org/groups/senior_lawers/resources/voice-of-experience/2024-september/the-evolution-of-voting-technology/ Accessed: October 20, 2024.

Lorch, R. S. (2001. *State and Local Politics: the Great Entanglement* (6th ed.). Upper Saddle River, New Jersey: Prentice Hall.

Panditharatne, M. and N. Giansiracusa. (2023). "How AI Puts Elections at Risk – And the N Needed Safegards." https://www.brennancenter.org/our-work/analysis-opinion/how-Ai-puts-elections—risk-and-needed-safeguards. Accessed: October 29, 2024.

Pazzanese, C. (2020). "Great Promise but Potential Peril." News.harvard.edu/gazette/Accessed: October 15, 2024.

PBS. (2024). "At Age 100 Jimmy Carter Casts His Ballot For the 2024 Election by Mail in Georgia. pbs.org/newshour/politics/at-age-100-jimmy-carter-casts-his-ballot-for-2024-election-by-mail-in-georgia. Accessed: October 23, 2024.

Pereira, I. (2024). "Tens of Millions of Early Votes Have Been Cast. What Could it Mean For Election Day? https/:abcnews.go.com/Politics/tens-millions-early-votes-cast-election-day-/story?id=115272249. Accessed: November 2, 2024.

Piechowski, D. (2018) "Technology Ethics and the Role of Government. "https://www.Businessofgovernment.org/blog/technology-ethics-and-role-government. Accessed: May 27, 2024.

Stratman, J. (2024). "Mayor Adams Corruption Trial is set for April 2025" nydailynews.com/2024/11/01/nyc-mayor-adams-corruption-trial-set-for-april-2025-judge/. Accessed: November 3, 2024.

Trish, B. A. (2024). "4 Ways AI Can be Used and Abused in the 2024 Election, From Deepflakes to Foreign Interference." https://theconversationstation.com/4-ways-ai-can-be-used-and-abused-in-the-2024-election-from-deepflakes-to-foreign-interference-239878. Accessed: October 22, 2024.

US Department of State. (2024). "Risk Management Profile for Artificial Intelligence and Human Rights." state.gov/risk-management-profile-for-ai-and-human-rights/. Accessed: October 25, 2024.

WSB-TV. (2004). "Secretary of State's Office Says They Stopped 240,000 Cyber Attacks Aimed at Crashing the Voter Website." https://www.wsbtv.com/news/local/atlanta/secretary-states-office-says-they-stopped-cyber-attacts-aimed-crashing-voter-website/ZMN5BK6LBZBNDA7BUB3ETBT34Y. Accessed: October 24, 2024.

ETHICAL BEHAVIOR IN OFFICIAL NEIGHBORHOOD ORGANIZATIONS

INTRODUCTION

This chapter brings us to an area of which local government ethical conduct is not often thought about. Although our focus is on local general-purpose government, there is another level of which many citizens may not always take notice. These are neighborhood organizations officially designated as a part of the local government. Such associations are normally written into the local general-purpose government's charter. (Note 1) Most are under the responsibility of a specific division of the municipality.

BELOW THE MUNICIPAL LEVEL OF GOVERNMENT: OFFICIALLY RECOGNIZED NEIGHBORHOODS

The lowest level of government in the American three-tiered federal system is normally assumed to be the municipal level. Local governments, however, do not always stop at this point. In several American cities, important policy proposals are made within the municipality's officially designated neighborhoods.

Private neighborhood associations are by far the rule in this country. There are however a few neighborhood organizations written either into a city's code of ordinances or into the actual city charter as in the case of Atlanta, Georgia with 25 Neighborhood Planning Units and 242 official neighborhoods. (Note 2) (atlanta.gov, nd) In addition to Atlanta, one finds officially designated neighborhoods in Birmingham, Alabama: 99 official neighborhoods (birminghamal.gov, nd); Cincinnati, Ohio: 52 official neighborhoods (Cincinnati-oh.gov, nd); and Arlington County, Virginia: 60 official neighborhoods. (Arlingtonva.us, nd) to name a few. (Note 3) Being written into the city charter gives these neighborhoods an legal standing to recommend and sometimes establish policy.

This chapter will consider ethical behavior in official neighborhood associations only. (Note 3) Using the notion of "government's obligation" as an indicator of whether or not a public entity is acting ethically, a question appears: have the neighborhood organizations, most notably the boards fulfilled their obligation to their residents as well as the municipality? As with all governmental entities, official neighborhoods are obligated to display the same ethical behavior. (Note 4) They also obligated to comply with laws including open records acts and the sunshine laws of their states. (Note 5)

It is important to point out that there is no evidence which suggests official neighborhood organizations are by nature unethical. Most do just fine. At the same time, it is always a good idea for urban citizens and the employees of the local city departments which are tasked with overseeing their neighborhood organizations to keep a close eye on their operation as they would keep an eye on any other division within the government.

As you read through this chapter, keep in mind the ethical obligation to all of its citizens. Is the local government making sure that their neighborhood organizations are always acting ethically themselves? Is the government itself always acting ethically towards its treatment of their neighborhood organizations?

LOCAL NEIGHBORHOOD ASSOCIATIONS ETHICAL FAILINGS: DEALING WITH UNEQUAL POLITICAL, AND ECONOMIC POWER AND GOVERNMENT POLICY

Unequal benefits of economic development

Neighborhood organizations are just as susceptible to ethical failures as any other government: "All community organizations have vulnerabilities" (Logan and Molotch, 2007, p.142). One of their vulnerabilities begins with the nature of those individuals who are more likely to become active in the neighborhood associations. The most active individuals tend to be the more affluent and educated citizens. The problem is that in many cases, this stratum of society has its own biases resulting in questionable ethical outcomes (Crenson, 1983, p. 139). It is because of this possible social and economic bias that decisions emanating from many community organizations, may run the risk of being made in the interest of middle-to higher-income residents often at the expense of lower-income individuals. Since every organization in the American polyarchy (public or private) is structured to achieve its political goals sometimes at the expense of other organizations, (Dahl, 1971) historically, affluent neighborhoods have been more successful than those with less wealthy residents in achieving what their political goals.

With greater political power in wealthier neighborhood associations less economic development is available for the entire municipality especially for citizens of poorer neighborhoods who often need the greater economic support. It becomes an ethical problem when the wealthier neighborhood associations are able to use their political power to syphon off available municipal funds which leads to the unequitable distribution of economic resources by governments to poorer neighborhoods, a violation of the obligation to all citizens. Since very few wealthy neighborhood associations oppose local economic investments. (Unless it impacts their own single-family residential housing.), they become parties to this sort of unequal investment and distribution of the local wealth.

Unequal land uses

In addition to manipulating the local government into a situation where wealthy neighborhoods are able to achieve a greater share of economic benefits, affluent neighborhood organizations have been quite successful specifically in promoting or rejecting land use issues. The use of land is considered the most important policy decision a neighborhood organization can make, the result has often been higher quality land uses in wealthier neighborhoods and unwanted land uses being forced upon economically lower scale neighborhoods (Logan and Molotch, 2007, p. 142). This being the case, local governments become a party to the unequal and thus unethical distribution of land use. With diminished political power, there is often little that a neighborhood association in a less wealthy part of the municipality can do to stop this. These neighborhoods wind up with the type of land uses one would not normally want. Unequal land uses may become what is sometimes called "environmental racism." The following case study is a fictional account of a local government's unethical behavior based upon a real incident.

CASE STUDY 9.1: A GOVERNMENT CONDONED UNEQUAL LAND USE

In the charter of one of the larger American cities, the official neighborhoods have been designated as "Municipal Neighborhood Districts (MNDs). There are thirty in all, each having a population of about 30,000. The districts are designated as MND-1, MND-2 … Through MND-30. Every portion of the city is located in one or another MND. Each is required to meet no less than once a month. The neighborhoods have been given very specific and important roles in the operation of the government. For example, all land use change requests, as well as liquor and restaurant licenses must first be heard by the MNDs. Although the districts may not have the authority to make law, they can propose policy. The city council can ignore their suggestions, which they do on a few occasions. The city council cannot take up land use and licensing matters until they receive the input from the neighborhoods.

The city geographically is longer east and west than north and south. The east side is clearly the wealthier part of the city. One can see neighborhoods having housing ranging from upper middle-class homes to large estates. Although there are some newer and well-kept neighborhoods on the west side, there is a great deal of substandard housing. Those neighborhoods also have a higher number minority populations. One also finds many more bars, liquor stores, shoddy convenience stores selling beer and wine, salvage yards, warehouses, and some small manufacturing plants. There are only two major chain supermarkets on the entire west side, all of which are in gentrifying neighborhoods. Except for a few liquor stores and even fewer bars, these land uses are not found on the east side.

In August of 2020, a 24-hour hyperstore was proposed for a vacant piece of property in MND-18, on the east side. The store planned to sell groceries, dry goods, and beer and wine. This particular hyperstore had a well-deserved reputation for being a hangout with poorly made goods. The store was definitely not wanted in the neighborhood. Unfortunately, the hyperstore company was a major worldwide corporation with a lot of financial backing. The residents of the eastside's MND-18 realized that they did not have the resources to fight the proposal, so they turned to some of the neighboring MNDs with the argument that if it happens here, it can (and will) happen in your MND. The only good news for MND-18 is that the proposal would require a change in zoning which gave them some chance to block the hyperstore.

When the rezoning proposal came before the city council, citizens from ten of the eastside MNBs were present. The council stenographer counted 123 residents wearing "Stop the Store" paper badges. During the public participation session at the council meeting, member after member told the council rather forcibly that the proposal would cause irreparable damage to the MNB. The counter argument was that the reputation was unjust and that the new hyperstore would be a perfect fit for the neighborhood. It would be well-maintained and would have well-made goods to sell.

In the end, the city council voted down the proposal. The property in question is today an upscale grocery store serving the residents of the nearby MNBs.

In the past few months, another property issue arose in the city. This time the proposal was on the west side. A developer went before the city's liquor commission to seek approval for another convenience store. This would be the fifth such store in a square mile on the border between MND-2 and MND-3. Ten women from the two MNBs did everything in their power to fight the proposal. Unfortunately for them, after the beer and wine license was approved by the liquor commission, the city council also approved the construction, saying that they had no legal authority to stop the store. The new convenience store was opened two months later.

- Was the outcome simply a matter of well-organized neighborhood political power? (Neumark, 2023, p.p. 37-50)
- Do you think that the city council really have no choice? After all, they turned down the hyperstore under similar circumstances.
- Did the city fulfill their public obligation to the entire population, or did they favor some neighborhood districts over others?
- Did the city council act completely ethically in disallowing one unwanted land use but allowing another?
- Are all the neighborhood associations in this city treated equally?
- If you were a member of the city council how would you have voted?

Unequal public policy: environmental racism

As ethically questionable as is Case Study 9.1, another very damaging real incident occurred in Flint, Michigan. High levels of lead were found in the city's drinking water, while the city and state completely ignored the horrendous health consequences with 12 deaths and 80 more residents sickened. (Booker, 2021) (Note 6)

Since specific land use policies are mostly under the jurisdiction of local governments, municipalities all over the country share the responsibility for perhaps the most unethical policy of all: environmental racism. It is an example of governmental policies which go beyond just the official neighborhoods. Such policies can have disastrous results in neighborhoods. In most cases the associations do not have the political power to fight it.

Environmental racism occurs when (mostly local) government policies intentionally allow the location of polluting and waste facilities in poorer neighborhoods, primarily in communities of color. It largely has and still persists because of policies and practices which favor the well-being of wealthier neighborhoods who have the ability to exercise political power over less wealthier neighborhoods. (Ihejirika, 2023) As one can imagine environmental racism results in disastrous health issues among the residents, particularly in younger children. This unequal treatment of neighborhoods is clearly unethical.by any standard of governmental behavior. (National Resource Defense Council, nd)

In some municipalities where environmental racism exists and neighborhood organizations are structured into the local government, the government becomes culpable in whatever discriminatory decisions they or their neighborhood organizations may make. In a pluralist democracy, one may expect that the give and take of the various organizations would lead to some organizational advantages. The government itself is one of the organizations. If one accepts the idea that government should be a neutral referee (Dahl, 1961), the ethical actions of the local government can be called into question by allowing subsidies, tax abatements, or changes in land use when it favors one community over another. When such favoritism exists both the local government and a specific neighborhood's actions can be regarded as self-serving. The most ethical governments are those which serve the entire community, wealthy and poor alike.

NEIGHBORHOOD ORGANIZATION MEMBERSHIP AS AN ETHICAL QUESTION:

Even though some neighborhoods are a division of the municipal government, a few associations are allowed to collect dues. If a citizen does not pay the dues, he or she is not allowed to vote on items which come before the association's board. Individuals are free to join or not to join as they see fit. The fee structure should never be arbitrary. If there is a fee to join, everyone should be expected to pay the same dues, with some reasonable exceptions such as those who may be retired.

Unlike in private neighborhood associations, the ethical problem may arise when these associations allow special discounts for certain targeted membership. Business memberships particularly have become important, and associations sometimes use discounted fees to entice businesses to join. Business members can be used to either support or quell opposition to some neighborhoods' proposals. The ethics of these discounted association fees can be questionable since some organizations simply attempt to buy off businesses to support or to not oppose a particular policy, generally something connected to land use. The ethical consideration arises especially if that business would not have ordinarily joined. In many cases, such business "contributions" are not properly vetted (Logan and Molotch, 2007, p. 39).

Whether ethical or not, in some cases neighborhoods may be forced to "play the growth machine game for economic reasons: the prosperity of the neighborhood organizations may require them to join with at least some of their business owner adversaries. (Logan and Molotch, 2007, p. 39).

The Bridge Highway case study below presents such an economic ethical concern. This fictional account is of a real recent dilemma faced by an official neighborhood association in an American city. Did the neighborhood take the ethical highroad?

CASE STUDY 9.2: THE PROBLEM WITH BRIDGE HIGHWAY

Bridge Highway is located in a middle to upper middle-income neighborhood in a large American city. This neighborhood, itself, is a textbook example of a quiet residential area with some multifamily and retail land uses along the edges. The highway is often thought of as the neighborhood's main street.

In every possible way, Bridge Highway is the complete opposite of the remainder of the neighborhood. The highway is known throughout the entire state and region as the center of adult entertainment, but not necessarily patronized from those who live in the immediate neighborhood, including a number of exotic dance clubs and "spas." As a result, of its adult nature, the highway has always served as an embarrassment to many residents of the neighborhood.

Because most of the adult entertainment venues do not own the land on which their establishments sit but are leased from a few large property owners, in 2021, the councilmember for the area proposed a city ordinance which would end the "grandfathering" that most of the clubs enjoyed. Accordingly, each club would be given five years to close. There were some constitutional concerns, since such an ordinance would appear to run counter to the *Ex-Post Facto* clause. However, the time given to these establishment would be enough to garner a profit, and this proposal was tried in another state and passed United States federal constitutional muster.

There was, however, significant opposition to the ordinance from other parts of the city. Quite a few other neighborhoods felt that such an ordinance was favoring the Bridge Highway community because of its upper income status. Many of their residents felt that they have similar problems which were not being addressed.

The board of directors of the official neighborhood association immediately approved the council member's proposal. In order to get this through the city council because of the opposition of some other parts of the city, the neighborhood association felt they needed both support from the "legitimate" businesses as well as a lot of additional funding needed for a lobbyist and or for a potential court case. Unfortunately for the neighborhood, there had always been very little business interest in joining the neighborhood association. In order to get business, buy-in the board decided to offer discounted neighborhood association membership to some "select" but not all business establishments. The assumption was that as a member of the neighborhood association, these businesses would be more likely to support the council member's proposal.

An ethical question was brought up, however, from one of the board members: there was nothing in the neighborhood association's by-laws that allowed them to offer discounted memberships. Such an action could be construed as arbitrary and capricious. Beyond memberships, the neighborhood association was also hoping to solicit contributions in addition to dues from the same businesses. Again, there was nothing in the by-laws which allowed them to do so.

The member believed that such arbitrary actions were unethical without a thorough vetting from the city's law department, such practices could get out of hand. The concerned board member proposed two policies to be included in the by-laws. The first would be to eliminate all discount memberships for any reason. The second would be to vet thoroughly any contribution from any source. (A list of relevant questions would have to be established.) Both policy suggestions were defeated by a wide margin. If the two policies were incorporated into the by-laws the association's board of directors believed they would not be able to get the needed business buy-in.

The proposed zoning ordinance was ultimately turned down by the city council. Although a few joined, no businesses remained as members of the neighborhood association, neither have the by-laws been changed.

(Neumark, 2023, p.p. 204-205

- If you were on the neighborhood board, how would you have voted?
- What decision about joining the neighborhood organization would you have made if you were a business owner on Bridge Street?
- Do you see an ethical dilemma in this case or is it simply a matter of elitism?

The above case study points out the same ethical dilemma that all local governments face: the good of the neighborhood versus making a questionable ethical choice. These dilemmas are not always easy to solve. There is a way that the local general-purpose governments can solve this dilemma by establishing their own policy including what is and what is not allowed by neighborhood organizations regarding the collection of dues, also putting a standard amount of dues paid by both the residents as well as the businesses within their jurisdiction.

Monitoring neighborhood organizations

There is another question regarding the board's actions in the above case study. Why did the city's department responsible for neighborhood organizations not step in, especially in light of the possibility of an ethical question? Even if one believes that the one dissenting board member was making too big of a deal over a minor neighborhood issue, the city's department could have been more astute. There is no record to indicate that any of the city's department employees, past or present, have ever met with the city's neighborhoods' leadership on this or any other ethical issue. This does not just concern Bridge Highway. When a city has an official neighborhood system, how closely should they be monitored? (The city in which Bridge Highway is located has over 150 legal neighborhoods, but it is not out of the realm of possibility that there can be yearly meetings between the responsible department and the neighborhoods' leadership. This particular city has not established any sort of oversight policy regarding their neighborhoods.

The problem is that many local governments simply do not have the resources to watch over their neighborhood organizations, even though their actions and decisions can have important ethical consequences. That also presents an ethical dilemma.

Accountability

The sort of decisions made by the neighborhood in the case study happen because of the lack of accountability. In some instances, only the top leadership of the organization's board is subject to the city's ethics code as in Atlanta's N.P.U. system. The remainder of the board as well as the general membership are not. Also, it is not always clear to whom official community organizations are responsible. City councils are responsible to the voters. Public department managers are responsible to either the city council or the municipal executive. It is not unusual, unless some misdeed comes to life, for neighborhoods to be accountable to no one but themselves even though they are responsible to their residents. Too many of the local citizens are apathetic, and if they know that such subgovernments exist at all (and many do not), these individuals do not see the importance of neighborhood associations. In the end, apathy allows questionable ethical conduct to continue.

CONCLUSION

Having neighborhoods with official legal standing is a good thing. These associations bring government closer to the people, even their role is limited to policy advisement. They are still important enough for a municipality to have adopted them into their charter or code of ordinances. It is imperative that the neighborhood association and local government all work together. With legal standing comes the responsibility to act ethically as is expected with every entity of the local government.

Local governments of course cannot control the economic realities of every neighborhood within their jurisdiction. There has always been an unequal distribution of both economic as well as political power since the founding of this nation. (Davidson, Gienapp *et al.*, 1996, p.p. 187 -196) They can, however, make sure that no matter where a neighborhood is on the economic ladder, that the services provided to its neighborhoods are provided equally. Not doing so makes the local government culpable for further institutionalizing this inequality.

The neighborhood associations themselves have an ethical responsibility to the general-purpose government as well as the remainder of the municipality's citizens. To that end, local governments must take decisive action to more closely monitor their official neighborhood associations. and they must take responsibility when these organizations are not acting ethically. Keeping a close eye on their subgovernments is an important step in the ethical obligations of our local governments. There must be a partnership. Unfortunately, the two case studies in the chapter suggest that is not the case. As this book has emphasized, ethical behavior is everyone's business.

NOTES

Note 1: The term "general purpose government" refers to the most common local governments which supply the majority of public services to residents. They include cities, villages, towns, townships, borough, Native American reservations (Lorch, 2001, pp 233- 265) and in some cases counties and the Louisiana parishes.

Note 2: The City of Atlanta has a two-tiered neighborhood system. In addition to the 242 official neighborhoods, there are twenty-five neighborhood planning units (NPUs) written into the city charter. Each of these planning units are comprised of a cluster of neighborhood based on their council district and approximately twenty-thousand residents. All land uses except for business licenses must first be herd on the NPU level before they go on to the city council. The city council is not obligated to agree with an NPU's decision; however, according to former Atlanta zoning administrator John Bell, in the majority of cases the council agrees with the NPUs' decision. The NPUs are a branch of the planning department. (Neumark, 2023; also see atlantaga.gov, nd))

Note 3: Sometimes it may be difficult to distinguish between a neighborhood and an independent city. Virginia-Highland in Atlanta is an example of a neighborhood with legal standing. In most cases, named neighborhoods are just that: named. Some neighborhoods are often thought of as separate cities but are actually a section within a larger city. One example is Hollywood, California which is a neighborhood within the city of Los Angeles. Another is La Joia, California a neighborhood in the city of San Diego. (Morrison, 2021) Brooklyn, of course, is a portion of New York City. Brooklyn also has legal standing as a separate county (Kings County) (ny.gov, nd)

Note 4: Most official neighborhoods do not have employees. Those who make policy for these subgovernments are resident volunteers. Since the chapter cannot address employee ethical behavior, it can still look at the policies emanating from these neighborhood associations to determine whether or not a specific action may be ethical according to the definition presented in this book.

Note 5: If you wish to find out if your neighborhood association is private or a legal entity within the local government, the municipal clerk should have that information available.

Note 6: The water crisis did not extend to Flint Township, a wealthier suburb surrounding the city. For a more compete discussion of the Flint Water Crisis, see Neumark, 2023 (p.p. 175 – 176)

CONCEPTS FOR THOUGHT OR RESEARCH

Accountability
Brooklyn (Kings County), New York
Code of ethics
Economic development
Environmental Racism
Ethical dilemmas
Ex-post Facto Clause
  (grandfathering)
Hollywood, California
La Joya, California
Legal (official) neighborhood
  organizations

National Resource Defense Council
Neighborhood planning Units
  (NPUs)
Neighborhood political power
Open records acts
Private neighborhood organizations
Government's obligations
Sunshine laws
Unequal distribution of a
  municipality's wealth
Unequal public services

REFERENCES

Arlington, Virginia. (nd) arlingtonva.us/Government/Projects/ Neighborhoods#:~:text. Accessed: November 8, 2024

Atlanta, Georgia. (2018, nd). http://www.atlantaga.gov./governments/ departments/City-planning/neighborhood-planning-units. Accessed: June 2, 2018 and November 8, 2024.

Birmingham, Alabama. (nd). birminghamal.gov/community-resource-officers-resources-crs/. Accessed: November 8, 2024.

Booker, B. (2021) Ex-Michigan Governor Rick Snyder and 8 others Criminally Charged in Flint Water Crisis. www.npr. org/2021/01/14956924155/ex-michigan-gov-rick-snyder-and-8-others-criminally-charged-in-flint-water-crisis. Accessed: March 12, 2022.

Cincinnati, Ohio. (nd). cincinnati-oh.gov/city-of-cincinnati/ residents/#:~:text. Accessed: November 8, 2024.

Crenson, M. (1983). *Neighborhood Politics.* Cambridge, Massachusetts: Harvard University Press.

Dahl, R. A. (1961). *Who Governs? Democracy and Pluralism in an American City.* New Haven, CT: Yale University Press.

*__________. (1971). *Polyarchy, Participation, and Opposition.* New Haven, CT: Yale University Press.

Davidson, J. W. and W. E. Gienapp, C. L. Hayerman, M. H. Lytle and M. B. Stoff. (1996). *Nation of Nations.* New York: McGraw-Hill, Inc.

Logan, J. R. and H. L. Molotch. (2007). *Urban Fortunes the Political Economy of Place.* (20th Anniversary ed,) Berkeley, California: University of California Press.

Morrison, P. (2021). "What City do you Live in? Don't Say Hollywood." https://latimes.com/California/story/2021-03-09/what-city-do-you-live-in-don't-say-hollywood. Accessed: June 15, 2024.

Neumark, G. (2023). *Civic Literacy Policy & Policy in the American City.* Dubuque, Iowa: Kendall Hunt Publishing Company.

Ny.gov. (nd). ny.gov/counties/kings. Accessed: November 9, 2024.

THE HISTORY AND DEVELOPMENT OF LOCAL GOVERNMENT CODES OF ETHICS

10

INTRODUCTION

From the beginning of our nation through the nineteenth century, American cities virtually had no ordinances as today's ethics codes. Although there were several reasons why urban ethics did not concern the American population, some of the more important were, first, we were not yet an urban nation. Most Americans lived outside of the major cities and had little interest in what happened there. The second reason was communication. Even if the interest was there, it was difficult to get an honest picture of how cities operated because of the shear distances and the lack of today's communication. Governments from local to national were much more out of sight from their populations. The third reason was not so benign neglect to downright hatred of cities from higher level government officials. Thomas Jefferson, for example, referred to cities as political ulcers in the United States. (Macionis and Parrillo, 2001, p. 70) Finally, many early American politicians believed that the United States was better than the same kind of corruption which was characteristic of European governments. Constitutional convention, Massachusetts Representative Nathaniel Gorham stated: "We have no rotten boroughs"! (Bowen, 1986, p. 121)

THE BREAKDOWN OF ETHICAL URBAN GOVERNMENTAL

Gorham couldn't be more wrong! Right from the beginning, Americans had felt negative towards their cities. To early Americans, cities were antithetical to basic American values. (Conn, 2024) As a result of these attitudes and a myriad of negative factors, most of the larger American cities eventually suffered from ethical government nightmares: this was the era of the political machines.

By the beginning of the 1900s many cities in the United States were deeply corrupt (Stephenson, 2020). Starting from shortly after the Civil War to about 1924, (Note 1) older established American cities experienced the greatest breakdown of any kind of ethical behavior among their officials that this nation had ever known (Jones, 2012, p.p.115–16).

There were a number of reasons why and when the breakdown began to happen:

- **Massive Immigration**: In a very real sense, massive immigration to the United States began around 1845 with the Irish potato famine. It is estimated that 1 to 2 million mostly impoverished individuals immigrated to this country. (History Place, 2000). The greatest number came to the northern United States port cities such as New York and Boston. Immigration to the larger cities also included the rural poor from other areas of the United States, looking for a way out of their economic misery. The number of immigrants was so great that the cities were not equipped to handle their swelling populations. At one point, 80% of New York City's population and 87 % in Chicago were comprised of immigrants. (Judd and Swanstrom, 2010, p. 30) Most knew nothing about local city governance which created a serious vacuum in urban leadership. The governance of many of the larger cities increasingly became out of control.
- **The Civil War**: In the 19th century wars called for increased industrialization which exacerbated urban immigration into the mostly northern cities. With the vast majority of immigrants being completely ignorant of urban culture and politics, those immigrants had no conception of the way policy and law were formulated in our cities. Because of this lack of knowledge, they were easy to manipulate by the corrupt machines.

- **State and national Indifference:** As an agricultural nation, cities were generally ignored. Agricultural interests held the majority in legislatures of every state, resulting in the indifference to the problems faced in their cities. Indifference was also the case emanating from Congress as well as from the White House. (Judd and Swanstrom, 2010, p. 38)
- **Lack of public social service infrastructure:** No public social services were available to needy urban residents. A few religious institutions and settlement houses provided a minimal amount of aid, but for most of the impoverished immigrants, there was nowhere to turn.
- **The acceptance of vice:** Since so many of the immigrants especially after 1850, escaped from corrupt and oppressive governments around the world, they accepted vice as normal as the only governmental system they knew. There was no understanding of any other way.
- **Jobs:** The strength of the urban political machines was their ability to hand out jobs to the loyalists. Jobs were seen as a reward for a person's loyalty to the machine. No training was required. Without a concept of ethical conduct, there was no thought of ethical behavior. At least their new city gave them a job. That's all that mattered.

All of the factors above created an urban governance vacuum. And into the vacuum came some of the most unethical characters in American urban history.

The historical Political machines were a hierarchical organization with a tightly organized clique, controlled by a single individual, normally called a boss. (Judd and Swanstrom, 2010, p. 197) In just about every case, the boss and **his** entire organization were corrupt. They were only concerned with the pursuit of wealth, and power from the control and distribution of the spoils of office. (England, 2003, p. 197) The urban political machine can be thought of as the process of exchanging favor for votes normally from organizations illegally in power. (Ross and Levine, 2012, p. 117)

A sample "Rogues Gallery" of infamous bosses and their political party affiliation includes:

- **William M. (Boss) Tweed of Tammany Hall** (D) (New York City) (Perhaps the most notorious of all the bosses.
- **George Washington Plunkitt** (D) (New York City)

- **Ed Flynn** (D) (Bronx County New York)
- **James Pendergast** (R) (Kansas City, Missouri)
- **Frank Hague** (Jersey City)
- **Big Bill Thompson** (D) (Chicago)
- **James Curley** (D) (Boston)
- **Hazen Pingree** (R) (Detroit)

(Neumark, 2023, p. 69; Lorch, 2001, p. 87)

The machines did do some good, especially helping immigrants who came here with nothing to obtain some of the basic necessities of goods. (Hinner-shitz, nd) (Note 2). In some cases, they controlled the governmental chaos that was already rampant in many American cities. On the other hand, they hurt a lot of people: stealing tax monies, extortion, even physical harm to their opponents. The question remains: do you believe that the ends justify the means? Corrupt and unethical behavior of the urban machine governments was not sustainable. Why? Something had to change, and it did. (Note 3)

REFORMS

The Reformers

Eventually, a series of reformers would come on the scene in an effort to end the local corruption. No matter what their own ethical failures, these urban reformers of the time were quite successful in bringing about such a magnitude of change in the structure of American cities as to result in local governments becoming significantly more modern and profession-al. (Jones, 2012, p.p.118–21) There were hundreds of reformers; however, four stand out in particular. (Note 4) They include:

- **Thomas Nast:** whose political cartoons ultimately brought down Boss Tweed.
- **Jacob Riis:** whose book *How the Other Half Lives* featured pictures of some of the worse living conditions in New York City. The book went nationwide, if not worldwide, and embarrassed the State of New York to the point where they were forced to become a party to the reform movement.

- **Jane Addams:** who developed a series of settlement houses (Hull House) to teach immigrant women all about American culture.
- **Upton Sinclair:** whose book *The Jungle* pointed out the horrible working conditions of mostly immigrants in the Chicago meat packing plants.

These four individuals along with the many others woke up the American population as well as the state governments which had heretofore ignored the plight of their cities, including government corruption, and the gravity of the local governmental ethical breakdown. The publicity forced the states to take more responsibility for the wellbeing of their local communities. The most important step was to allow and encourage local governments to enforce anticorruption ordinances.

The Reforms: making local governments more ethical

As a result of all of the forces that brought down so many American cities, the concern of the reformers, and the beginning of the age of scientific government, state governments started to take a real interest in the plight of their downtrodden cities. States all over the country passed enabling legislation which allowed cities to restructure their governments to the modern cities one sees today. Taken together, the new urban governmental structures have helped produce our more modern professional and ethical cities. Some of the reforms more directly related to insure ethical behavior include: (Note 5)

- **Strong Mayor:** (Note 6) During urban political machine times, the machine controlled the mayor. One of the starkest examples is Boss Tweed. Tweed controlled the City of New York, but he was never the mayor. Although most bosses were mayors, this did not always the case. With a strong mayor, ethical responsibility is nested in one individual, unlike the weak machine era mayors, where it was not always clear who had the authority and responsibility for the laws and policies. Was it the mayor? The board of aldermen? The boss? Or some combination? With this reform those responsible for ethical political actions became more transparent.
- **Professional city (county) manager:** (Note 7) This is one of the most important reforms. Under political machine rule the only qualifications to be mayor, besides loyalty to the machine, was the ability to breathe.

Since local elections were rigged, anyone who the machine wanted to be mayor, became the mayor. It was not necessary for the mayor to have any political experience or understanding of the job of mayor. Although a city manager is neither elected nor a mayor, an individual chosen for this position must be educated in professional public management.

- **Civil Service:** The majority of local public servants must prove their abilities through civil service. This may include a test, certification in their area of expertise, or a degree from a university or college. Cities can no longer simply appoint the mayor's brother-in-law, or a loyal machine member who knows nothing about the service rendered by the department. Even appointed top level commissioners have a proven background in their specific area of administration. (Note 8) In order to attract the best local employees, most local governments have put a system of tenure seniority into place. (Judd and Swanstrom, 2010, p. 78)

- **City councils and at large city councils**: Although the difference between a board of Alderman as practiced in machine dominated cities is nuanced, there are some differences between boards of aldermen and modern city councils. Aldermen wards were generally smaller and less professional than Today's councils. Legislators are known as council members. Because of the graft and corruption associated with the old-style political machines, many municipalities have changed their designation of wards to districts. The term "ward" has taken on a more pejorative meeting. A few cities, such as Chicago, still call their representative districts wards.

Some cities have gone to an at large city council. Although normally found in smaller cities. The value of one single municipal wide legislative district is that it breaks the close personal relationships between the urban legislators and their constituents that were necessary in order for the machine to work. The alderman often posed as a friend as if the alderman was doing personal favors for the residents of their wards. They may have been, but at a price! This reform forced an at large council candidate to become more professional: not only were there more competition, but a candidate's professional background was the only way a voter could judge whether or not the individual would make the best choice. The candidate had to present him or herself as the most professional and ethical in order to win over an entire municipality. (Note 9)

One additional difference, which however was more a product of the time period, was that the term aldermen meant "men." Today, of course, municipal councils as well as public non-elected public employees are comprised of men and women who are chosen for their positions because of their ability to perform their tasks.

- **Term limits**: A more recent reform includes term limits. In this case an elected individual will be only allowed to serve a limited number of years. In some cases, that person can come back and serve another two terms after being out of office for a term. The concept of term limits is to make sure that an individual does not build up such a constituency that no matter what unethical lapses may occur, that person remains in office. It also allows for fresher ideas to circulate through government.
- **Non-partisan and odd year elections.** Since the urban machines were supported by one or the other of the major political parties, an important reform was to break that connection by having local elections moved to odd number years where there are no regularly scheduled national partisan elections. The candidate could no longer ride the coattails of a particular political party. The other obvious move is to simply remove the party label of a local candidate.

ETHICS CODES TODAY

The establishment of codes of ethics

At the same time that the dominance of political machines was waning, the American population began to view political and public administrative offices as a public trust. The concept of trust became increasingly supported by local governments attempts to control their own unethical behavior: a higher level of ethical decision-making became established as the norm from those in public office. The idea that governments should be acting in the public interest was catching on. (Spector, 2021) In order to support ethical behavior among their employees and officials, local communities throughout this country have now established codes of ethics.

Formal codes started off slowly. In the beginning municipalities adopted codes only when citizens felt the need for them. (Potrzebie, 2023) One of the earliest attempts at establishing an ethics code was in New York City. (Davies, Leventhal, and Mullaney, 2023, p.p. 49-53) Ironically, at the time such notorious characters as Boss Tweed, and his Tammany Hall Organization. The codes did very little to curb the corruption. In 1922, the State of Alabama also adopted an ethics code. (Jones, 2012) Considering Alabama's Jim Crow laws, it would appear that the ethics codes of 1830 and 1922 were both quite meaningless.

The earlier attempts at the establishment of municipal codes of ethics had to be more limited, because so many local governments were, and still are, subjected to state policies. Federal and state governments were able to impose fines, issue reprimands, or even dismiss employees who violate codes of conduct. It was more difficult for the local governments to do so. (Lorch, 2001, p. 369) This also has been changing. As states have passed the necessary enabling legislation, more municipalities are establishing the modern specific ethic codes one sees today. Today's codes state clearly and comprehensively what is included in public ethical behavior. (Wechsler, 2013, p. 17). At the same time, codes must also insure fairness in their administration if the public is to support such actions (Cox, 2004, p. 10).

How well ethics codes are successful also depends on the culture of the local government. (See Chapter 5) Organization structures are malleable: rules are sometimes bent, procedures are ignored, formal channels of communication are altered by informal relationships, and individuals act on personal values and not the ethos of the organization. (Denhardt, 1994, p. 19) If the administrators or boards tasked with the enforcement of their ethics codes display a pattern of unethical behavior such as nepotism or favoritism as well as an inconsistent administration of their ethics codes, their employees are also possibly likely to do so. (Note 11)

Ethics officers and enforcement

The most common administration of municipal ethics codes is handled by an ethics officer and his or her team. The best functioning department is completely independent from of all other divisions of the government including the council and mayor. The idea of the responsibility for enforcement is also evolving. Not all local governments, even those with strong

ETHICAL BEHAVIOR IN AMERICAN LOCAL GOVERNMENTS

ethics codes have or should have ethics officers. (Gross, 2021) (Note 12)
The lack of an actual officer does not mean that codes cannot be enforced.
Each department, for example, can be responsible for its own enforcement.

A well-working ethics system should also have developed a mechanism for
the public or other employees to report unethical behavior. It should be
made easy and safe to do so.

Problems

- **Effective reporting system:** An effective reporting system is not always the case. In a recent study, researchers found that only 55 percent of the local governments which responded to a survey concerning
  their ethics enforcement indicated that they even have an established
  process in place for reporting ethics issues. (ICMA, 2019)
- **Unclear authority:** Since every local government is different in regard
  to enforcement, it is unclear how or which office has the authority to
  penalize those officials who have displayed some unethical behavior.
  The question is still open regarding the independence of an ethics officer from municipality to municipality.
- **Lack of nationwide standards:** There is no single set standard of ethics codes and enforcement. Local governments' set of ordinances may
  range from the very detailed to a code which more closely resembles
  an outline, or they may simply rely on their state's laws as their own.
  Sometimes, ordinances are made with a great deal of thought and are
  reviewed in an ongoing basis. In some municipalities, additions are
  made as the need arises: a city may discover that a certain unwanted
  act from an employee is not covered by their ethics code, so it is simply
  added to cover future cases.

The good news

The good news is that ethics codes have become the rule in the vast majority of our local municipalities. While the urban reformers, and the
early ethics codes were not and are not perfect, they have gone a long way
in making modern local governments much more professional, ethical as

well as responsible to their citizens. Local governance is a partnership. As this book noted all along it is also the responsibility of the citizens to be a partner with their local government.

PROFESSIONAL URBAN GOVERNMENT MANAGEMENT

With all of the reforms and modern technology, local government has become clearly more professional. Has professionalism eliminated ethical lapses? Unfortunately not, but public employee honesty has come a long way since the days of Boss Tweed.

From the beginning of a prospective public manager's journey through a career in public service hiring is most often handled by professional human resources professionals. Someone vying for a public service position must demonstrate knowledge of what the duties and expectations are before that person is hired. Through the entire process, the ethical expectations are also made clear. Urban government professionalism is now expected in all aspects of our American experience. (Tindall and Shi, 1996, p.p. 1004-1006).

Public management has now become a branch of social science over the years. Likewise, ethics is an important aspect of the scientific approach taught in universities: the more scientifically and professionally trained, the more honest and ethical are government employees' actions. Even though participation in local governments may be low, citizens are more aware of what transpires in their governments. Professionalism as well as citizen awareness are increasingly emphasized in today's public management courses of study.

CONCLUSION

Modern municipal ethics codes were in a very real sense born out of the ethical breakdown of local governance from just after the Civil War until about 1924. The Civil War exacerbated massive industrialization and immigration from workers from all over the world, including other parts of the United States, particularly in the northern coastal cities.

In addition to rapid industrialization which seemed out of control, was the attitude of Americans towards their larger cities which went all the way back to the founding of the United States. Thomas Jefferson was well known for his distain of American cities. (Phillips 2010, p. 425) As essentially an agricultural nation, rural dominated state governments also shared in the dislike and mistrust of their urban areas, In many cases, states ignored their cities. For these reasons, a governmental vacuum was created in many of our larger American cities.

Someone had to govern. Those someones were a collection of the most dishonest, corrupt, and unethical rogues one could imagine: the early urban political machines. The machines were fueled by the massive movement of immigrants into the cities, most of whom had no conception of American government and politics. Although the machines did some good for the immigrants, that good came with a price. Those downtrodden people were largely taken advantage of by the machines.

With the advent of federal immigration laws in 1924 as well as the publicity from a series of urban reformers, the era of machine dominance came to an end. A problem still remained: how could cities protect themselves from corrupt machine politics happening again? Fortunately for the future of the cities, the states started to take notice of what was transpiring and passed laws enabling cities to restructure their governments in an attempt to end the widespread machine corruption. The result was the creation of the modern American cities' governmental structures replete with codes governing public ethical behavior. (Note 12)

One of the most important aspects of the modern city is the professionalism of our government employees. Hand in hand with scientific and good government movements was the development of professional education, such as the Master of Public Administration degree: the more professional the employee, the less likely he or she will practice unethical behavior.

Along with professional education, municipalities established codes of ethics. Starting off slowly as guidelines of employee conduct, local ordinances eventually became the modern specific codes of ethics.

The refinement and enforcement of the codes are still evolving. All in all, our country's local government are among the most ethical world-wide. We can be proud of the ethical behavior of the majority our local government officials.

NOTES

Note 1: The exact date that American urban corruption started can be debated; however, the more specific year 1924 is used as the beginning of the end of the corrupt urban political machines. It was in 1924 when the first of the important federal immigration policy and laws were passed, including the Quota System. Because much of the local corruption was aided by immigrants who did not understand the American legal system, the machines were able to take advantage of them. Once the first wave of immigration gave way to the second-generation American born individuals who were educated in this country and understood the true meaning of the urban machines, they had a more difficult time victimizing American immigrants.

Note 2: The good the machines did was for a price: normally for votes.

Note 3: Unethical government behavior did not start with the urban political machines or even in the urban areas. Even some of our well-known "founding fathers" displayed behaviors which were unethical by today's standards. One such laps of ethics involved Manasseh Cutler. In 1787, Cutler was the main investor in the Ohio (land) Company. He used his influence with Congress to speak in person to several representatives of the constitutional convention, including Strong, Gorham, Madison, Mason, Martin, Williamson, Rutledge, Charles Pinckney, and Hamilton. (Bowen, 1986, p. 181) He Had already manipulated Congress into protecting his investment in the large swath of land by lobbying for the Northwest Ordinance. Cutler did not have to lobby too hard since several congressmen were already investors (conflict of interest). Since he could make a great deal of money with his land deals, he had to make sure that nothing in the development of the constitution served to hinder his financial interests. (Concordia University Centers for Civics Education, 2024) He had no difficulty gaining access to the above representatives, including inviting Cutler to their homes (Bowen, 1986, p. 182)

Cutler's efforts almost bared fruit. On August 28, Rufus King was able to have the majority of the convention agree to what would became the Northwest Ordinance. It wasn't until the end that Delegate Gouverneur Morris, was able to have that clause deleted. (Bowen, 1986, p. 183) Eventually it passed Congress but not the constitutional convention.

This case presented several unethical behaviors. The first is the conflicts of interest, second how easy it was for Cutler to obtain entry into the very secretive constitutional convention and be accepted socially into the homes of several delegates.

These actions from our incipient government do not excused the later actions of the urban political machines; however, it is meant to show how fragile ethical decisions were emanating from public officials right from the beginning of our country. The unethical decisions happened quite readily because so many citizens in 1787 were very much uninformed about what Congress and the convention were doing.

Note 4: The same argument can be made for any number of reformers who were not mentioned. The author chose the particular four reformers because of the great impact they made not only on society as in the case of Jane Addams and Upton Sinclair, but also directly impacting machine politics and making our local governments more professional and ethical.

Note 5: Not every municipality has adopted all of the reforms. Over the years local governments have chosen which of the reforms are the most important.

Note 6: A strong mayor is one with a great deal of centralized authority including hiring and firing professionals. A weak mayor may have some executive authority but is more likely found in those municipalities with a manager who has the real authority in managing the day-to-day operations.

Note 7: Most larger municipalities with a diverse population have not adopted a professional manager form of government. The concern is that since most professional managers have historically been drawn from the Caucasian middle class, that person would have less understanding of the politics and cultures which make up many of the larger municipalities, causing that individual to be biased towards only one segment of the population leaving out minority communities in the policy decision making process. Middle sized and smaller cities which may have less diversity are more likely to have a professional manager. This is now changing and an increasing number of minorities are now going into urban public management.

Note 8: This reform is not foolproof. Just because one is an expert in a specific area of service does not preclude unethical public behavior. Recently, the finance and water commissioners in a major American city were sentence to prison for graft and corruption. Both were experts and well experienced in their respective work of their commissions. They were also ordered to pay back the city for any lost revenue because of their questionable actions.

Note 9: Some cities have gone to a hybrid legislative form. In these municipalities, there are both council districts as well as a smaller number of at large representatives. Whether from a district or the entire city, all council members have the same authority.

Note 10: As unlikely as this sounds, this author has witnessed firsthand these actions from a local government's ethic board.

Note 11: As a counter point, Gross (2021) suggests that some cities do not need ethics officers. There may be better ways of enforcement without a separate department.

Note 12: Of course unethical behavior of some public employees still exists. The codes, however, have served to keep unethical behavior to as much of a minimum as possible.

CONCEPTS FOR THOUGHT OR RESEARCH

Anti-urbanism	*How the Other Half Lives*
At large elections	Hull House
Boards of Aldermen	Immigration
Boss	Industrialization
City Council	ICMA (International City Managers
City (County) Manager	Association)
Civil service	Jacob Riis
Codes of conduct	Jane Addams
Conflict of interest	Manasseh Cutler
Corruption	Master of Public Administration
Ethics codes	Northwest ordinance
Ethics commissions (boards)	Professionalism movement
Ethics officers	Progressivism
Government as a public trust	Public administration

Quota System

Reformers

Scientific Management

State indifference to cities

Strong mayor/weak mayor

Term limits

The Dichotomy

The Jungle

Thomas Jefferson

Thomas Nast

Upton Sinclair

Urban governance reforms

Urban political machines

Wards

William (Boss) Tweed

REFERENCES

Concordia University Centers for Civics Education. (2024). "Convention: a Daily Journal Sunday July 15, 2024. cui.edu/centers-for-civics-education/convention-a-daily-journal/post/sunday-july-15-1787. Accessed: December 2, 2024.

Conn, S. (2024). "The Anti-Urban Tradition in America: Why Americans Dislike Their Cities." Blog.oup.com/2014/10/anti-urban-tradition-america-cities/. Accessed: November 16, 2024.

Cox, R. W. III. (2004). "The Profession of Local Government Manager: Evolution and Leadership Styles." In C. Newell (ED.) *The Effective Local Government Manager* (3rd ed). Washington, DC: ICMA.

Davies, M., S. Leventhal, and J. Mullaney. (2023). "An Abbreviated History of Government" laws_ny_state_/history_govt_ethiclaws_davies_pt2.pdf. Accessed: June 19, 2024.

Denhardt, K. G. (1994). "Organizational Structure as a Context for Administrative Ethics." In T. L. Cooper (Ed.). *Handbook of Administrative Ethics.)* New York: Marcel Dekker. p.p. 19-182).

Demir, T. (2001). "Politics and Administration a Review of Research and Some Suggestions." https://www.fau.edu/spa/pdf/Dimir_PoliticslandAdministration_New_MS.pdf. Accessed: June 28, 2024.

Fscj. (nd). "The Growing Pains of Urbanization 1870 – 1900. Fscj. pressbooks.pub/modernushistory/chapter/the-growing-pains-of-urbanization-1870-1900. Accessed: November 18, 2024.

Gross, S. (2021). "Ethics Codes For Local Governments, Part 1: Considerations, Scope, And Applicability." https://mrsc.org/stay/informed/mrsc-insights/february-2021/ethics-codes-for-local-government-part-1. Accessed: July 4, 2024.

Hinnershitz, S. (nd). "Were Urban Bosses Essential Service Providers or Corrupt Politicians?" https:/billofrightsinstitute.org/activities/were-urban-bosses-essential-service-providers-or-corrupt-politicians. Accessed: June 24, 2024.

History Place. (2000). "Gone to America." historyplace.com/worldhistory/famine/America.html. Accessed: November 19, 2024.

ICMA. (2019) "Incorporating Ethics Into Everyday Work In Local Government." https://www.icma.org/blog-posts/incorporating-ethics-every-day-work-local-government. Accessed: July 4, 2024.

Jones, M. D. (2012). "The City Governs Political Science." In R. Steinbacher and V. O. Benson. *Introduction to Urban Studies* (4th ed. pp 115-130). Dubuque, Iowa: Kendall Hunt Publishing Company.

Judd, D. R. and T. Swanstrom. (2010). *City Politics the Political Economy of Urban America* (7th ed). New York: Longman.

Lorch, R. S. (2001). *State and Local Politics: the Great Entanglement* (6th ed.). Upper Saddle River, New Jersey: Prentice Hall.

Macionis, J, J, and V. N. Parrillo. (2001). *Cities and Urban Life* (2nd ed). Upper Saddle River, NJ: Prentice Hall.

Neumark, G. (2023). *Civic Literacy Policy and Politic in the American City*. Dubuque, Iowa: Kendall Hunt Publishing Company.

Phillips, E..B. (2010). *City Lights Urban-Suburban Life in the Global Society* (3rd ed.) New York: Oxford University Press.

Potrzebie. (2023) https://ask.metafilter.com/370129/how-common-is-it-for-municipalities-to-have-a-code-of-ethics. Accessed: June 27, 2024.

Ross, B. H. and M. A. Levine. (2012). *Urban Politics cities and Suburbs in a Global Age* (8th ed). Itasca, Illinois: Peacock Publishing Co.

Spector, S. J. (2021). "Ethics Matter -Ivy Lee and the First Code of Ethics.: https://www.globalalliance.org/Thoughts/2021/2/19/ivy-lee-and-the-first-code-of-ethics. Accessed: June 27, 2024.

Stephenson, M (2020). "A History of Corruption in the United States." hls.harvard.edu/a-history-of-corruption-in-the-united-states/. Accessed: November 18, 2020.

Tindall, G. B. and D. E. Shi. (1996). *America a Narrative History* (4th ed.) New York: W. W. Norton & Company.

Van Riper, P. P. (1989). "The American Administrative State; Wilson and the Founders." In R. C. Chandler (ed). *A Centennial History of the American Administrative State*." New York: The Free Press. P.p. 3-36.

Weschler, R. (2012). "Local Government Ethics Reform." *National Civics Review*, 101 (3). P. p. 26-30.

THE ETHICS ROLE OF THE LOCAL INSPECTORS GENERAL

11

INTRODUCTION

When one thinks of ethic officials in a local community, that position normally belongs to an ethics officer. However the ethics role of local inspectors general is included in this book because in some cases, public employee ethics investigations may also be within the role of the inspector general. (LII, 2024) In addition, since every local government have differing structures, it is sometimes difficult to tell where the authority of an ethics department ends, and that of the inspector general begins. Since some of you may wish to become an inspector general the following chapter discussion will address some of the questions about their ethics role. (Note 1)

Conflicts

At a superficial glance, the two positions, ethics officer and inspector general, may appear to serve some of the same functions: For example, both offices have the authority to conduct investigations of conflict-of-interest laws and other ethics' laws and regulations. (The Association of Inspectors General, 2024) Depending on the degree both are impowered to identify and investigate fraud, waste, abuse of employee's public positions, and corruption. (Atl Oig, 2024) The best way to think of the two positions is as a continuum. As the employee's misbehavior becomes more serious the investigative authority goes from the ethics department to the office of the inspector general.

POINTS OF CONFLICT

Since there is not always a discrete boundary between the authority of each office territorial conflict can ensue. The following are points of potential conflicts:

- **Scope of investigation**: An inspector general may investigate minor violations, which should be left off to the local ethics officer (E.O.)
- **Investigative approach:** I.G.s normally have more aggressive and more widespread investigative authority, including subpoena ability. (Fewer E.O.s have that authority.)
- **Unclear reporting structures**: Each office may report to different leadership levels and different departments. The levels and departments may themselves conflict with each other.
- **Mutual Investigations**: Each of the offices may wind up investigating each other.

(Based on information provided by Google.com, 2024)

GOVERNMENT SUPPORT AND POLITICS

An office of public ethics is expected to provide direct support to the investigators from the various governmental inspector general offices. (Shaub, 2015) This is the case on all governmental levels. However, it does not always work as efficiently on the local level. As is often the case, when some local communities have both positions, and only one reporting system to file a complaint, it is up to the ethics officer to refer the more serious cases to the inspector general. To the extent that a case first has to start out in the ethics office begs a judgement call which may or may not be accurate.

The questions then arise: is it an ethics offence? A criminal offence? Or
both? If the two offices do not support each other, that process can have
its rough edges.

Politics

For those of you who will become an inspector general, it is important that
you are aware of the politics. As with every other aspect of local government, sometimes political considerations come to the surface. In the fictionalized case study below, based upon a real political incident, the large
urban county in question at first had no intention of creating an Office of
Inspector General until the state threatened to take away its prize position,
its train station. The state claimed it had the right to do so because of alleged corruption in the city government. The county countered by creating
an Office of Inspector General to root out these alleged ethical evils. Thus,
the game of ethics' politics began.

As you read through Case Study 11.1, keep in mind that an inspector general is supposed to be totally apolitical. The irony since is that the office
of inspector was created out a clear political consideration and continued
until the end.

CASE STUDY 11.1 WHERE ETHICS MEET POLITICS:

Chaos Creek is a very highly populated urban county. Its most prized
position is its train station, which is owned by the county and run under the transportation commission, a branch of the local government.
The Grand Union Station is not just a small regional train station. It
is a major national and international all-purpose station, known by
travelers from all over the world. Besides the actual train platforms,
the station includes a three-story shopping mall (the largest in the
state), and a twenty-story hotel. It is also a national transportation
hub with interstate and commuter trains; as well as local, regional
and interstate buses, and the largest subway station in the Midwest.

Unfortunately, the management of facility has been rocked by one ethics scandal after another, including bribes and nepotism in the past several years. There had been so many corruption allegations that the state had been trying to come up with ways to take the station away from the county and just looking for reasons to confiscate the station. (The real fact is that the state wanted very much to have the station as its own.) In 2022 the state came very close to doing just that. They came within two votes of assuming ownership of the station. (Note 2) Among some legislators, their position has been that the county has not been doing enough to address the corruption issues.

Although this county has an active and completely independent ethics manager and ethics commission, dealing with the serious nature of the train station's corruption issues has been beyond the scope of the ethics department's authority. The cases were, however, being investigated by both the state and federal law enforcement.

To make matters worse, there were also constant local media reports about the ethical behaviors of various Grand Union Station managers. This led to the general public having had serious doubts about, not just the station, but the ethical behavior of entire local government. Unrelated, several of the former County's C.E.O.'s political appointees to other departments have been under a federal corruption investigation and to this date six of these individuals have been sentenced to federal prison. The C.E.O. herelf has never been charged with any wrongdoing, although the public doubts that this can be going on without her knowledge. There was obviously a crisis of confidence in the county government.

Feeling the heat of the state's attempt to take over the station, a newly elected C.E.O. instituted an ad-hoc committee to study how the county can forestall the states attempt to pull in the reins of the train station but also to look at the entire scope of corruption within the municipal government. (The C.E.O. chose not to use the ethics commission to study the county's ethics problem, perhaps because ethics commission and he already had some friction between when he was a county commission member in the past.) The committee would then report directly back to him with their recommendations.

The most important recommendation of the ad-hoc committee was to establish the position of Inspector General (I.G.) with the ability to investigate and apply punishment to the more serious ethical and criminal lapses. To that end, proposed legislation was sent to the county commission to set up an inspector general's office. The proposal went through the legislative process quite quickly and became an ordinance only three months after the initial *ad hoc* committee was instituted.

It is in the context of this legislation where friction developed. Perhaps this came about because of some of the changes. The county already had a very active and successful ethics apparatus. The ethics commission would be essentially the same with a few additions. It would be expanded from five members to nine and would now have the authority to govern both departments.

The real beginning of problems came about when under the ordinance, the ethics department was placed under the newly hired Inspector General. (Note 3) The ethics commission, now officially renamed "The Chaos Creek County Inspector General/Ethics Commission" (I.G.E.C.) retained the authority to hire the ethics manager as well as the inspector general. The ethics manager and inspector general were given subpoena authority, but it was taken away from the commission. All final decisions would be made by the I.G. or the ethics manager with appeals authority given to the commission. They could only affirm or negate decisions already made by either of the two departments. An important element of the new structure is that both the ethics office and the I.G. will remain completely independent of all other branches of the municipal government.

Over time, things have not gone so well among the two offices and some elected officials. Not only has friction developed between the mayor's office and the inspector general, but also between the ethics office and the I.G. The administrators of each of the offices disliked each other. The distain was clear during joint I.G.E.C., ethics manager, I.G. meetings.

The relationship between the inspector general and the C.E.O.'s office became so acrimonious that recently, a new *ad hoc* commission was set up by the C.E.O. and county commission to **investigate** the operation of the I.G.'s office. (The ethics manager put all the blame on the IG for bringing on this investigation.) He vehemently suggested that his own ethics department itself was completely faultless and ran perfectly. (Note 4) Clearly, these personal differences were not in the best interest of the county. The actual professionals, however, under the officers were able to work together as needed.

There were some bright rays of hope for the inspector general including the complete support of the I.G.E.C. Hundreds, if not thousands of community written letters in support to the county commission and C.E.O. (The ethics officers refused to write a supportive letter.) And even the county's city's largest newspaper wrote editorials supporting the I.G. At first, the county commission seemed to be taking a lukewarm position regarding the Inspector general.

Over time, the tide turned against the I.G. Ultimately, the IG along with the entire board, except for one individual, resigned. The inspector general blamed, in part, the ethics manager's acrimony.

As of now, the county C.E.O. has dismantled the entire I.G.E.C. New legislation has now severely diminished the authority (and ability) of the office of the inspector general. A temporary I.G. has been hired, but the ethics/investigative system is currently in chaos. (Note 6)

- Do you believe that the county would have decided on their own to spend millions of dollars in tax moneys to develop this whole new branch of government if they had not felt threatened by the state?
- Could they have simply increased the authority of the ethics manager and the commission which were already in place?
- Since the C.E.O. and the ethics commission already had some friction among them could this have been a way of getting the commission off of his back? And if this were the case, was it ethical to create this office, spending millions of dollars, strictly for that political purpose?
- Why do you think that the county commission did not give the ethics officer additional authority to look into the matter of awarding a contracts to questionable vendors?

- What in your opinion were, if any, the governmental ethical failings to be found in case study 11?

The citizens of the county may never know what the real politics were behind the creation of this new branch of local government as well as the reorganization of the ethics office and commission. Both the ethics commissioner and the Inspector General were both doing excellent jobs. But as this case study points out no position, even the ethics or Inspector General's office, is entirely free of politics.

Looking at Case 11.1 from a political perspective

The purpose of this chapter is to look at the ethical behaviors surrounding the development and role of the local government's inspectors general. There are clearly many local municipalities which take the establishment of their inspectors general with the utmost seriousness and for the betterment of the community. However, in some cases as represented by the true events in Case Stude 11.1 that is not always what ones finds. All governmental policies are products of politics. (Every one of us in our own way is a politician.) (Laswell, 1936; Neumark. 2023, p. 14) The case study is not meant as a critique of politics. Indeed, every policy development process is imbued with politics. (Note 7) It is only when political considerations cause unethical behaviors that it becomes problematic. The most important ethical question is did the county commission and the C.E.O. make decisions which did or did not serve the best interest of the municipality. Were those decisions made by rational well thought out policy in the best interest of all of the citizens of the county?

If you feel uneasy about the politics and ethical issues brought up in the case study, you should. The political manipulations are certainly not uncommon. Many questions still remain:

- Was this the most ethical solution to a real problem that the county could come up with?
- Was diminishing the authority of the I.G. ethical?
- How ethical was the role of the ethics manager in this debacle?
- Should the county have considered the possible outcome? After all, the ethics officer was entrenched in his position for years. Would the new inspector general become a partner or a rival?

- Was the reorganization a backdoor way to dissolve the ethics commission itself?: is it possible that the county commission, the C.E.O. and/or some important governmental individual were upset with the commission because of previous ethics investigations and possibly hitting too close to home?
- Did the reorganization come about as a result of a reasonable give and take of the entire county community inside or outside of the government?
- Did politics prevail over ethical considerations?

Although a fictionalized version of a real incident, the Grand Union case study is representative of any local government anywhere over any political/ethical issue in this country. All governments have an ethical mandate to make the most ethical decisions. There is no reason why politics should interfere. It must be the position of the local government to make sure that this does not happen.

THE EDUCATIONAL FUNCTION OF THE INSPECTOR GENERAL

In those communities where both an ethics officer and an Inspector General are expected to work together they share an educational function to teach employees all about the ethical expectations of their employment. They are also both responsible to access how well professional employees understand the ethical standards of conduct (Office of Inspector General, 1990). An inspector general can be a valuable asset to the ethics apparatus of a community. In many cities the inspector general sponsors regularly scheduled meetings with the local government employees and even with the interested general public to explain the laws and policies governing items such as contract compliance, contract bidding, corruption, and expected public behavior. Although many local citizens do not always think about this as a role of an I.G., ethical education is one more important components of the job of their functions.

CONCLUSION

The overall missions of the inspector general and ethics officer are not the same; however, their functions can overlap. In some of the more serious cases of public employee unethical behavior, it isn't always clear whether the investigation should be handled by an ethics officer or the local inspector general. The most common joint interest area is in the investigation of conflict of interest and in determining which department gets which cases. In addition, they are also expected to support each other when facing political opposition.

Even though both the ethics and inspector general offices are supposed to be completely independent, politics can become and became a part of their establishment and operation. Case study 11.1 points out an irony: how an inspector general's position became available in a real case involving a large American county because of political considerations and how political and ethics considerations are destroying that position.

The question is not whether or not politics should exist in the development and operation of an I.G. department. The fact is they are there and enter into every aspect of public decision making.

As an individual possibly studying to become an inspector general in the future, it important that you continue to be aware of this reality. In the above case study the circumstances under which the position of inspector general was created, and its continued operation has caused a great deal of damage to the further ability of the office of the I. G. You must be aware and forestall they types of hindrances.

Finally, one of the important aspects of the inspectors general's position is ethics education. The I. G. may join with the ethics officer to educate employees as well as the general public on ethical behavior within the municipality.

The work of local inspectors general is very important to the well-being of our communities. Staying independent but working hand in hand with the ethics department, the local legislature and the municipal executive to insure that our local municipalities continue to be well run is really the ethical component of a local inspector general.

NOTES

Note 1: The City of Atlanta provides one example of the convergence of the ethics department and that of the inspector general. Both offices are governed by the same board. They also use the same telephone number for the public to report what they consider an unethical or illegal behavior by a city employee. Whether this structure or complete independence of the two are the most advantages for the ethical operation of the city is still an open question depending on their ability to work together.

Note 2: The question of the legality of such a takeover and the state assuming the bond indebtedness was never discussed.

Note 3: In this case study the ethics department being placed under the authority of the inspector general was highly unusual and led to a great deal of friction.

Note 4: The I.G.E.C. met with the two officers on several occasions in an attempt to solve their personal animosity, but to no avail.

Note 5: One of the commissioners refused to sign any of the support letters. Interestingly, this individual ran for an elective office in another jurisdiction before she moved into the county and accepted an appointment to the commission. There has been speculation that she may now wish to run for an elective office in this city, which could be why she would not sign the letter.

Note 6: Several employees of the I.G.E.C. have now filed suit questioning whether or not the county C.E.O. has the jurisdiction to disband the I.G.E.C. The case is pending.

Note 7: Who gets what where and when is a common definition of politics used by political scientists from Harold Laswell's 1936 classic book of the same title. Neumark adds an additional broader definition to Laswell's statement: "politics can be defined as the attempt to determine who get what, why, when, where, and how." If one accepts Neumark's definition it is very easy to see that all of us from time to time are engaged in politics. We are all politicians! There is nothing sinister or unethical about trying to get our way. The words "politics" and "politicians" are given a pejorative meaning only when doing so is attempted for some unethical purpose.

CONCEPTS FOR THOUGHT OR RESEARCH

Conflicts between inspectors general
and ethics officers
Conflict of interest
Conflicting authority
Ethics education
Government support of ethics'
departments
Government support of inspectors

general
IG (inspector general)
Political considerations in
developing policy
Public policy
The ethical role of inspectors general
Unclear investigative authority
"We are all politicians"

REFERENCES

Atl Oig. (2924). "Ourt Mission & Vision-Atlanta OIG." https://atloig.
org/about. Accessed: December 4, 2024.

Google.com. (2024). google.com/search?q=conflicts+between+inspec-
tors+general+and+ethics+officers. Accessed: December 4, 2024.

Laswell, H. (1936). *Who Gets What, When, and How.* New York: Whit-
tlesey House.

LII Legal Information Institute. (2024). "Government Ethics Responsibilities of Inspectors General." Law.cornell.edu/cfr/text/5/2638.106.
Accessed: December 3, 2024.

Neumark, G. (2023). *Civic Literacy Policy and Politics in the American
City.* Dubuque, Iowa: Kindall Hunt Publishing Company.

Office of Inspector General. (1990). "Ethics in Government." Jttps://oig.
hhs.gov.,oei/Reports/oei-02-90-00710.pdf. Accessed: January 9, 2020.

Shaub, W. M., Jr. (2015). https://www.oge.gov/web/oge.nsf/Resources/
OGE+and+the+Inspector+General+Community. Accessed: July 9,
2024.

The Association of Inspector General.org. (2024). inspectorgeneral.org/
institutes/institute. Accessed: December 11, 2024.

AN OVERVIEW OF PUBLIC ETHICAL BEHAVIOR: CONTINUING CHALLENGES AND OPPORTUNITIES

12

INTRODUCTION

Reading through this book on public ethics one might think that too many public organizations are dysfunctional and operate with questionable ethics especially compared to private organizations. There is no evidence, however, to support this conception (Note 1) Public organizations are not perfect, and mistakes do happen.

Most municipalities operate with diligence in spending the public's money, developing trust, executing thoughtful policies, assuring legal operation, and maximizing the public good. There are obvious benefits to local constituents that accrue from transparent ethical organizational behaviors. Ethical government operations result in more efficient, lower cost governmental operations.

The problem is that one well publicized ethics violation can cast a cloud over the entire local government. (Widner, 2019, p.29) Such behaviors are often in the spotlight. Not only are unethical behaviors damaging to public organizations, in turn they are damaging to the public. One mistake may cause damage, but is eventually forgotten, but continued unethical behaviors could result in greater employee turnover, difficulty in recruiting the most talented individuals, and wasted public resources. (Jurkiewicz, 2013, p. 25) Would you be hesitant to join a public organization if some ethical failure in the past has come to your attention?

WHY SOME LOCAL PUBLIC EMPLOYEES EXHIBIT UNETHICAL BEHAVIOR

One may ask why do some public (as well as private) individuals act unethically? They do if they perceive some substantial benefit for doing so. Examples of unethical behaviors in public organizations include

- Groupthink
- Personal financial profit
- Outside influence
- Kickbacks
- Career advancement.
- Poor ethical education in ethical conduct

(Jurkiewicz 2013, p.27)

Unethical or ignorant leadership

One of the most common reasons is poor leadership itself which allows dysfunctional behaviors. Either the leadership is ignorant as to what is going on with their employees, poorly trained, or they just do not care. In the majority of cases, well trained aware leadership results in smoothly running and highly ethical organizations.

CONTINUING CHALLENGES

As most of us know, ethics and compliance are increasingly covered in the media. Because of the ongoing publicity, the public's perception of low ethical standards among government organizations is still strong. Rarely does one read about well-functioning ethical public organizations. In today's modern world with incredible advances in communication, the question still remains why are some local governments still facing ethical challenges:

Lack of enforcement tools:

The control of unethical behavior in many local public agencies may not be entirely complete. This is especially true in smaller local governments. (Lorch, 2001, p.369) To a greater or lesser extent many municipal governments lack the resources to catch misbehaved employees. (Note 2) The federal and state levels, which have the tools at their disposal, are able to impose fines, issue reprimands, or even dismiss employees whose actions are unacceptable. (Lorch, 2001, p.369)   Ethics departments may have to work with smaller staffs, may not have the sophisticated technology found on the higher levels, and are more under the control of the municipal legislature. (See Chapter 8)

Besides not having the resources, some simply lack the will to enforce these policies. And even if they have the will, being a closer level of government of the public, (Newman, 2016, p.p. 19 -23) they may have some political misgivings not found on the more separated higher levels.

Good ol' boys:

In some local municipalities, especially in rural towns, the so called "good ol' boys' network pervades their governments. (City-Data.Com, 2021) One finds "government for the few by the few." (Wallace, 2007) In some ways the good ol' boys' network is similar to the old corrupt political machine, although perhaps less sophisticated and organized. When a "member" of the network governs unethically, which "friend" is going to root that person out?

Organizational culture

The structure and culture of a public organization itself can present a challenge to the ethical behavior of some employees. Organizational culture and behavior are intertwined to produce "shared values, beliefs, assumptions, perceptions, norms, artifacts and patterns of behavior." (Ott, 1998, p.1) The connection becomes obvious when an organization is able to control its employees' behavior by shaping their cognitions and perceptions of meanings and realities. (Ott, 1998, p.69) Once again, this may be more prevalent is smaller communities.

It is not difficult for an observer to see the strong connection between organizational culture and behavior. (Neumark, 2012, p.6) If a culture tolerates unethical behavior, there will be unethical behavior. If the administrators of an organization display a pattern of unethical behavior, those individuals below the executive level are themselves likely to display the same pattern of behavior.

Even with the most comprehensive and well-designed structure, organizations are malleable which leads to rules being bent, procedures being ignored, and formal communication channels being altered by informal relationships. Officials who are determined to act on values different from those expressed from the formal organization can usually find ways to do so" (Denhardt, 1994, p.169).

Public employees are not doomed to follow the negative example of their administrators. Most public employees go about doing their jobs to the best of their ability, who clearly know the difference between right and wrong. Indeed, 40 percent of all workplace unethical behavior is reported by fellow employees. (Kemp, 2024) The percentage among public employees is even higher with 52 percent. (Rosenberg, 2008). Perhaps we would wish it to be higher, but many employees do not want to be considered "Whistleblowers." This also is one of the ethical challenges faced by our local governments.

OPPORTUNITIES

There is good news. Whether or not it is because of the electronic revolution, newspaper accounts, or instant reports and commentary from the electronic press, "Society is demanding greater integrity of character in its leaders" (Northouse, 2007, p.20).

In spite of the lower than completely satisfactory percentage of unethical behavior reporting, public organizations are aware of the perception and are continuing to address them. In light of the negative view, or perhaps because of the publicity, this has become an excellent time for local governments to contemplate and improve upon how their employee behavior is projected: "Large cities, such as Washington, D.C., Jacksonville, Florida, Atlanta, Georgia as well as many smaller cities, counties and towns across the country, have created or improved their codes of ethics over the past year" (Weschler, 2012, p.26).

Most local officials take these codes seriously. Acceptable norms of public behavior have become critical (Cox, 2004, pp. 3 – 4). Even among those local governments which have not adopted formal codes of behavior, many have published behaviors to be avoided. These include "bribes, forgery, leaking confidential information and influence peddling" (Lorch, 2001, p.369).

Continuing Municipal Reform:

Local governments have found other ways of ensuring higher standards of employee ethical behavior. The demise of the political machines in American cities was under way, city after city began the process of developing government reforms including ethics policies. Two particular local reforms stand out: the establishment of the professional city (county) manager and the breaking of the link between partisan political machines and the local government apparatus by moving local elections to odd years and eliminating political party involvement. In the majority of American cities, local elections are now held in separate years from national and state elections. The even year election cycle allowed the political parties' perpetuation of the urban political machine. Urban voters, many of whom could neither read nor write, simply voted a straight party ticket, keeping the machine in power. The other strategy is the non-partisan election. In this case, local election candidates run without any official party affiliation (On the other hand, it is often well known to which political party a candidate belongs).

Today, it is axiomatic that elected officials as well as professional urban managers, including mayors and city council members, should not align themselves with special interest groups including political parties (Svara, 2004. p. 40). Some local governments have adopted both of these reforms, while others have chosen one or the other. As a public employee, are there any additional reforms that you would like to see adopted by local governments?

University courses and professional local government

Public administration as an independent discipline started out as a course of study within political science but broke away in 1887 during the middle of the urban machine age. (Wilson, 1887) Although it took a while to catch on, the concern with professional management came about as a result of our increasing orientation to many aspects of science, including Frederick Taylor's "Scientific Management" as well as in the process of governance. (Neumark, 2012). At the same time the United States was moving into the "progressive era." (Davidson, Gienapp *et al,* 1996. pp. 591-621) The Good Government Movement and greater public awareness were an outgrowth of both forces. Professional management's goal on the local level was to separate urban governance from its political orientation because of the popular belief at the time that all local politics were inherently corrupt. This view of the total separation of policy and politics came to be known as the "dichotomy" (Henry, 1989, p.41). As the apolitical view grew in strength, an increasing number of local governments turned to the city manager as a more professional way of running the city. (Note 3)

Because, as written in chapter 10, the majority of larger American cities are more socially and culturally diverse which favors the electoral process over professional appointments, one finds most local government managers in medium to smaller cities. In the past few years, there are, however, a growing number of larger cities which have adopted the manager-council form of government, including Dallas, Texas; Charlotte, North Carolina; Phoenix, Arizona; Colorado Springs, Colorado; and Cincinnati, Ohio These cities have been able to work out a cooperative arrangement between the manager and mayor.

A last word about reforms

The above municipal reforms are just that: reforms. They may help to make local governments more professional; however, they are not a panacea. Cities are free to pick and choose all or none. All urban areas have their share of problems. The hope is that the more professional a local government may operate, the more ethical that municipality will be. This leads us to the most important element of all: you!

OUR ROLE AS LOCAL CITIZENS

Systems

One way of understanding the role of local citizens regarding ethical public employee behavior is through a political systems model. (Easton, 1953) The idea of Easton's concept is based upon a physics system model. (inputs -> analysis -> outputs -> inputs -> ...) We as Americans (if we choose) are a part of a series of many political systems including our own local governments. In a democratic society, all of our governments are constantly receiving policy suggestions (inputs), whether through elections, the media, town hall meetings, and/or personal messages to our government officials. Based on the various forms of communication, they consider what are the wants and needs of the public (analysis). They then make decisions or policy adjustments based on those inputs (outputs). As the adjusted policy receives additional inputs, the process starts all over again, and on it goes.

American municipalities typically receive inputs from all kinds of sources, but most important of all from its citizens, especially those who are alert to the actions of their public leadership. (Note: 4) It doesn't matter whether or not you plan to become a public servant, as a citizen, you have an important role in your local government's system.

Whether or not you subscribe to the systems model, there are some definite actions you can take to insure the best governance possible. First, be aware of your local government's codes of ethics. Codes of ethics should be easily accessible. If not, let your government officials know.

Awareness

The democratic operation and culture of public organizations also present an ethical challenge. Are the goals of government worth bypassing the democratic means? Although Americans expect our government operations to adhere to our democratic values, we all know that not every public organization is not and cannot always be run this way. As with private sector organizations some local governments and their branches have a top-down culture. There are those of course which must operate secretly for security reasons. Most Americans accept that many public organizations cannot always completely operate openly and democratically, but do not accept the organizations whose culture allows blatantly dishonest employee behavior.

Notice to what extent your municipality has adopted the good government reforms. Progressive urban reforms are certainly not perfect; however, they help to make modern government much more ethical and responsible to the citizens.

Communicate

Communicate with your local government employees. Get to know your public officials. Don't just contact them with a gripe. Let them know who you are and share ideas about good government with them. They may be busy, but a good government employee should always have the time for the constituents.

The suggestions may sound idealistic, but they are not. It is a part of your role as a citizen: "Ethical inquiry cannot be separated from the 'publicness' of the role and obligation to the citizenry" (Ventriss, 1994, p. 199). In the end, it is up to you to continue the awareness of your municipality's political structure. Awareness along with participation are the most salient keys to controlling unwanted public policies.

The continuation of a democracy brings about responsibility. Americans expect their government to be transparent and trustworthy, but these very qualities, produce a dilemma: not only are the American governments open to the citizens, they are also open to those who would try to influence government decisions for their own purposes and not necessarily for the good of rest of the population. Be the influencer for the good.

NOTES

Note 1: Although there has not been definitive research as to what percentage of American local governments may be purposely unethical, it is fair to say that most government employees follow the ethical approach to their public service. (Pelissero, 2023)

Note 2: Local authorities and districts are also included in the term local municipalities. They present an additional problem since especially authorities have non-elected boards and are often hidden from the public view.

Note 3: In reality the belief in total separation of professional management and politics is a fallacy. City managers are constantly having to deal with political issues. Unfortunately, many universities have not emphasized this point enough in their public management courses. Without the complete knowledge of the political side of urban governance puts professional leadership at a disadvantage. All too often, a manager will run into some political pitfall without being aware of the "hidden" politics which is one of the reason why the average tenure of a city manager is only 6.9 years. (Yamashita, 2005) So many of them have become embroiled in some political landmine.

Note 4: This is only a model. In reality local governments do not always listen to or act on the wishes of the local population. On the other hand, the more one is involved in the government, the more that the policy wishes of private citizens becomes credible.

CONCEPTS FOR THOUGHT OR RESEARCH

Codes of conduct

Codes of ethics

Corruption

Democratic political system

Good Government Movement

Good ol' boys

Non-partisan local elections

Odd year local elections

Organizational culture and
dysfunction

Organizational structure

Political landmines

Professional local government managers

Progressive era

Public Administration (public management)

Scientific Management

The role of modern communication

REFERENCES

City-Data.com. (2021). "How Common is Small Town 'Good Ol' Boys' Politics." city-data.Com/forum/rural-small-town-living/3270354-how-common-small-town-good-ol.html. Accessed: December 16, 2024.

Cox, R. W. III. (2004). "The Profession of Local Government Manager: Evolution and Leadership Styles." In C. Newell (Ed.) *The Effective Local Government Manager* (3rd ed.) Washington DC: ICMA.

Denhart, K. G. (1994). "Organizational Structure as a Context for Administrative Ethics." In T. L. Cooper (Ed.). *Handbook of Administrative Ethics.* New York: Marcel Dekker. P.p. 169 – 182.

Easton, D. (1953). *The Political System.* New York: Alfred A. Knopf, Inc.

Davidson, J. W. and W. E. Gienapp, C. L. Heyrman, M. H. Lyttle, M. B. Stoff. (1996) *Nation of Nations A Concise Narrative Of The American Republic.* New York: McGraw-Hill, Inc.

Henry, N. (1989). "The Emergence of Public Administration as a Field of Study." In R.C. Chandler (Ed.). *A Centennial History of the Administrative State.* New York: The Free Press. P.p. 37 – 85.

Jurkiewicz, C. L. "The Anatomy of Ethical Dysfunction." 2013. H. G. Frederickson, and Sharp. 23-41.

Kemp, A. (2924). "Most Unethical Behavior Goes Unreported and Unresolved." gallup.Com/workplace/648770/unethical-behavior-goes-unreported-unsolved.aspx. Accessed: December 18, 2024.

Lorch, R. S. (2001). *State & Local Politics: The Great Entanglement* (6th ed,). Upper Saddle River, New Jersey: Prentice Hall.

Neumark, G. (2006). Atlanta: classroom lectures.

__________, G. (2012). "The Atlanta BeltLine: a Cultural Clash – The Case of Tenth and Monroe." *Politics and Questions.* P. p. 1 – 26.

Newman, H. K. (2016). "Citizenship in our Local Community." In G. Neumark. *Citizenship in the Local Community.* Dubuque, Iowa: Kendall Hunt Publishing Company.

Northouse, P. G. (2007). *Leadership Theories and Practice* (4th ed.). Thousand Oaks, California: Sage Publications.

Ott, J. S. (1998). *The Organizational Cultural Perspective*. Chicago: Dorsey Press. In Pelissero, J. (2023). "Five Common Conflicts of Interest and How to Prevent Them." scu.edu/government-ethics/resources/five-common-conflicts-of-interest-and-how-to-prevent-them. Accessed: December 15, 2024.

Rosenberg, A. (2008). "Study: Ethical Breaches Becoming Common in Government." govexec.com/pay-benefits/2008/01/study-ethical-breaches-becoming-common-in-government/26192. Accessed: December 18, 2024.

Svara, J. H. (2004). "Achieving Effective Community Leadership." In C. Newell (Ed.). *The Effective Local Government Manager* (3rd ed.). Washington, DC: ICMA. P.p. 21 – 56.

Ventris, C. (1994). "The Publicness of Administrative Ethics." In T. L. Cooper (Ed.). *Handbook of Administrative Ethics*. New York: Marcel Dekker. P.p. 199 – 218.

Wallace, J. (2007). "Local Government Replaced by Good Ol' Boy Network. goldcountrymedia.com/news/60593/local-government-replaced-by-good-ol-boy-network/. Accessed: December 16, 2024.

Weschler, R. (2012). "Local Governmnent Ethics Reform." *National Civics Review*, 101 (3), 26-30.

Widner, R. (2019). "Ethical Conduct in Local Government." chrome-extension://efaidnbmnnnibpcajpcglclefindmkaj/https://www.cirsa.org/wp-content/upload. Accessed: December 14, 2024.

Wilson, W. (1887). "The Study of Administration." *Political Science Quarterly*, 2 (2).

Yamashita, E. (2005). "City Manager Tenure: What's the Average"? https://hanfordsentenial.com/News/city-manager-tenure-whats-average/article. Accessed: July 12, 2024.

EPILOGUE

Since this book was started in 2024, there have been some changes and updates in many of the case studies since presented in the chapters. Although almost all of the studies have been fictionalized and exaggerated, they are based on real incidents which have come to the attention of this author. These incidents have been reported in his own municipality, but also from cities and counties from all over the United States. The following are some of the case studies' updates:

- In Case Study 1.1: Club is still operating. The neighborhood suspects that the "new" owners are a shadow management.
- In Case Study 2.1: The case was significantly slowed down. It is now on hold, possibly to the end of the current president's term. There is a good chance that they may be dropped altogether.
- In Case Study 3.1: The C. D. C. decided not to pursue the request any further.
- In Case Study 3.2: The real private cities all received varying amount of tax hikes.
- In Case Study 3.3: The mayor has finished the prison sentence but has pretty much stayed out of the public eye.
- In Case Study 5.2: The BeltLine is up and running through the lot in question; however, most of the remainder of the lot is still a parking lot or empty.

- In Case Study 6.1: One of the two proposed BRT lines has hit a serious construction delay due to the previously undiscovered buried infrastructure.
- In Case Study 9.2: Bridge Highway is still problematic. There have two fires set by "urban campers" which had entirely destroyed the two bridges on the highway, each taking a significant amount of time to rebuild, further chasing the legitimate businesses out of the area. On the good side, there has recently been new multifamily residential construction along with a gourmet grocery store, which the neighborhood residents are hoping to serve to bring the road back to life. There has been no change in the neighborhood's membership policy, however. Also, none of the Bridge Highway businesses remains as members.
- In Case Study 11.1: The city has made major alterations to the ethics as well as the I.G. commissions. Both offices as well as the commissions are now totally separate. There is still only one citizen's complaint telephone number, and they are still expected to work together.